Better to Travel Hopefully

Better to Travel Hopefully

Father David's Diary in Ilkley
2005–2006

David Hope with Hugh Little

DARTON · LONGMAN + TODD

First published in 2007 by
Darton, Longman and Todd Ltd
1 Spencer Court
140–142 Wandsworth High Street
London SW18 4JJ

Unless otherwise indicated, scripture quotations are taken from the
New Revised Standard Version Bible, © 1989, Division of Christian
Education of the National Council of the Churches of Christ in
the United States of America.

ISBN-10   0-232-52704-0
ISBN-13   978-0-232-52704-9

A catalogue record for this book is available from the British Library.

Designed and produced by Sandie Boccacci
Set in 11.25/14pt Bembo
Printed and bound in Great Britain by
Cox & Wyman Ltd, Reading

For Hermione, Richard, Helena and Mathilda —
the Church of tomorrow.

Contents

Acknowledgements

The photograph of Father Tickle is reproduced by kind permission of Hull Daily Mail Publications Ltd.

Thanks to the Ilkley Gazette for permission to reproduce four photographs.

'The Spider', 'The Gnu' and 'The Rhinoceros' by Flanders and Swann are by permission of the Estates of Michael Flanders and Donald Swann. Enquiries: leonberger@donaldswann.co.uk

Words of 'The Landlubbers Song' by Ruth Wills © 2004 Scripture Union, used with permission (from the Landlubbers Holiday Club Programme).

'Our God is a Great Big God' by Nigel Hemming and Jo Hemming © 2001 Vineyard Songs (UK & Eire)/ Administered by Copycare, PO Box 77, Hailsham, BN27 3EF, UK. Used by permission.

'If I Were a Butterfly' by Brian Howard, © 1974 Mission Hills Music/Administered by Copycare, PO Box 77, Hailsham, BN27 3EF, UK. Used by permission.

Thanks to Virginia Hearn and everyone at Darton, Longman and Todd; Anne Kilvington and John Rainforth at St Margaret's; my wife Linda, April Salter and Claire Marshall for their encouragement. A special thanks to Ian Briggs, who rounded up the sheep on the back cover.

Above all, thanks to God for Father David!

HUGH LITTLE

December 2006

Preface

God moves in a mysterious way his wonders to perform. I don't need William Cowper's hymn to teach me this – I learned it from the Provisional IRA.

In February 1974 I was working as a reporter at the North of England Newspapers office in Darlington when reports came in of an explosion on the M62 near Leeds. The target was a coach carrying soldiers and their families from Manchester to Catterick. Twelve people died and many others were injured.

The atrocity stirred deep feelings at Darlington, only a short distance from Catterick. My first thought on hearing the news was: 'IRA – these are *my* people you are murdering.' The second was: 'I must get ordained.'

A wave of lengthy public-sector strikes had depressed the national mood in the early 1970s. Now, looking round at the gloomy faces of my colleagues in the newsroom, I told myself: 'Christianity is the only real answer to wickedness – I want to offer people hope.'

I suppose, now, that this was a kind of prayer.

By chance an invitation came to study Theology at Oriel College, Oxford, while my vocation was tested. It was during a visit to St Stephen's House theological college that I first met David Hope, the Principal. In contrast to the detached (often boring!) Oxford dons, he was committed to mission, warm and welcoming. Above all, he was interested in me! I was only with him for half an hour, but sensed that here was someone with a very special destiny.

It was astonishing to learn, more than 30 years later, that

Archbishop David Hope was to become priest-in-charge of my local church, St Margaret's, Ilkley. Having realised several years previously that my vocation lay in writing rather than as a priest, I asked if I could keep a diary with him about his time at Ilkley. He agreed straight away.

The world is much more dangerous today than ever it was during the IRA's terror campaign, although my conviction about the solution to evil is unchanged. All the same, it is still with considerable surprise that I can say to you at last: 'Readers, I offer you hope – David Hope.'

HUGH LITTLE

Introduction

Which book would you choose to take to a desert island? When Sue Lawley asked me this question in November 2005, I selected the Complete Works of Dickens. The request was refused – perhaps she thought I might use the paper as part of a raft (and, once afloat, aim *Oliver Twist* at a half-full shark). Instead, I selected *Pickwick Papers*. It's a pity I couldn't also at least have had *David Copperfield*, with that 'very 'umble person', Uriah Heep, because (unlike the obnoxious Heep) I really was humbled 40 years ago while being ordained as a priest in Liverpool Cathedral. Despite being excited, I felt small in the vastness of the cathedral. There was awe, too, in reflecting on the infinitely greater majesty of God:

> ... who sits above the circle of the earth,
> and its inhabitants are like grasshoppers.
>
> (Isaiah 40:22)

I had no long-term plans, but was content to do God's will where I was.

It was a privilege later to become Bishop of Wakefield, Bishop of London and Archbishop of York, but I trust that I developed no delusions of grandeur. Curate, vicar, dean, bishop, archbishop – all are mere channels of God's grace and love. And didn't Jesus turn the world's standards upside down (especially 'celebrity') by declaring that:

> ... all who exalt themselves will be humbled, and those who humble themselves will be exalted (Luke 14:11)?

Life at Bishopthorpe Palace was often like being on a tread-mill. Long hours, countless meetings, a huge volume of post and e-mails, forever being 'on call' … In my rare times of peace and quiet, I sometimes wondered whether this was what I had been ordained for.

I always wanted to conclude my ministry as I began it, as a parish priest. The 'higher' you are in life, the more you are cut off from your roots – as many a politician has found. Jesus spent most of his ministry surrounded by ordinary people, sharing both their joys and griefs and leaving his followers an example of service ('I am among you as one who serves' – Luke 22:27). The Church is called to be in the midst of people and, as I see it, the priest is a personification of what the whole Church should be and do.

Although there was little time to 'stand and stare' at York, at the back of my mind was the idea that on reaching 60 I should begin to look for a parish. I thought more about the idea in 2003, but by then other people had come into the equation. Rowan Williams had only just succeeded George Carey as Archbishop of Canterbury and it was clear that I should remain at York until he had settled in.

I first visited St Margaret's, Ilkley in April 2004, to dedicate a large painting by local artist Graeme Willson called *The Madonna of the Moors*. This features Mary and Baby Jesus with John the Baptist and St Margaret of Antioch in front of present-day Ilkley Moor – suggesting that Jesus is not just a character from history, but present today where ordinary people are. As well as the painting, I was struck by the church's beautiful stained glass and the choir. I felt I would be at home in a church where the Eucharist is celebrated almost daily and the Sacrament is reserved. As someone who enjoys walking, it would also be a pleasure to live only yards from Ilkley Moor, with the Yorkshire Dales close by – not that I expected much spare time!

On 1 August 2004 it was announced that I was to retire as

Archbishop early in the New Year and become Priest-in-Charge of St Margaret's. The announcement came on Yorkshire Day – an occasion treated seriously by a sizeable number in the county, but probably ignored by more. The timing was coincidental: I am pleased to have been born in Yorkshire, but am not a 'professional Yorkshireman'!

Rowan Williams suggested that I take at least three months off before starting in my new position, but in fact I only had one. St Margaret's parishioners had been without a priest for long enough, and both they and I would have been disappointed not to be together at Easter. Much of my four-week 'break' was taken up by packing and all the usual duties involved in moving.

St Margaret's was packed for my licensing on 2 March, when David James, the Bishop of Bradford, paid tribute to the considerable number of Christians in the Diocese who were making great sacrifices for their faith. 'Sometimes,' he said, 'I want to kiss the ground they walk on.' Within a few weeks, I was paying tribute in St Anne's Roman Catholic Cathedral, Leeds, to a man famous for kissing the ground at airports the world over – Pope John Paul II. Within hours of his death, there had been a clamour for him to be given the title 'John Paul the Great'. But, as I pointed out in the address, the Gospels remind us that:

> such greatness only comes from the recognition of one's whole dependence on Jesus Christ: Christ's strength in our weakness.

St Margaret's parishioners gave me the warmest of welcomes – perhaps being dazzled somewhat by the media spotlight. Fortunately, most soon regarded me more like another fixture and fitting. Shortly after the licensing, I attended a choral concert. One church member, realising I didn't know how hard the chairs are here, handed me a cushion. 'Many people who regularly come to our concerts like to bring their own cushions with them,' she said pointedly. After that, I was left to fend for myself!

The Acts of the Apostles examines the birth of the Church through what at times seem to have been rose-tinted spectacles – 'All who believed were together and had all things in common ...' (Acts 2:44). About a generation later, the picture of church life is more familiar:

> Now I appeal to you, brothers and sisters, by the name of our Lord Jesus Christ, that all of you should be in agreement and that there should be no divisions among you ... (1 Corinthians 1:10)

I am not surprised by the occasional mild grumbling at St Margaret's – but *am* impressed by the willingness to air any differences openly without allowing bad feeling to develop afterwards. As I suggest in the diary entry covering the Annual Meeting, the readiness of the minority to accept the majority view on a potentially divisive issue is an example to the wider Anglican Church.

Within a few days of my arrival, I was having fun in the deep end that is St Margaret's Playtime, a lively parents-and-toddlers group. I soon found I *was* able to be closer to people than as Archbishop. Deb and Phil Allen were ecstatic as I christened their 'miracle' baby, Louis, at Pentecost. Six days later, I proved I could still conduct a wedding, and it was a privilege in April to take the funeral service of Alec Smith, a man of great faith. These, and many similar occasions, brought considerable personal fulfilment.

A diary is not like a novel, which is more organised –

usually with what used to be called an introduction, main content and conclusion. Real life is often haphazard, and doesn't always develop in the right order! A diary is more like a series of photographs taken from different angles. The Bible is like that: it contains thousands of snapshots of God but, taken together, the *overall* impression is that GOD IS LOVE.

Better to Travel Hopefully contains hundreds of snapshots of my life in and outside St Margaret's, but the theme lies in a phrase of the poet George Herbert: 'Heaven in ordinary'. To me, everything conveyed by these words starts with God, Creator of all that exists. Heaven is all about us – in the things we see and the people we meet. There's a divine spark in every human person. True, it can be disfigured and marred by sin, but the potential is there in all of us. 'Heaven in ordinary' took on a deeper meaning when God showed his amazing love by entering our humanity as Jesus, to share our joys and sorrows, loving us 'to death' – his death. Through waiting on his love and taking it out, we can ensure that God's Kingdom gradually *does* come and his will *is* done on Earth, as it is in Heaven – at least in our own private worlds. What the future holds for the whole world lies in his hands – and underneath its sorrows are the everlasting arms.

DAVID HOPE
Ilkley
All Souls Day, 2006

+ Since the completion of this book, the sad news of the unexpected death of our treasurer and churchwarden, Barbara France, has reached us. We recognise the immense contribution she has made over the years to St Margaret's, and pray that she may rest in peace – and rise in glory! DH

✿ SPRING –

Let Them Eat Cake

March

❧ Tuesday 1 March

Of all Jesus' stories, few are as dramatic as that featuring two brothers, the older of whom goes bananas when his sibling squanders his inheritance on gin and girls but receives a banquet on returning to his doting father. The lad is the first in a long line of prodigal sons and daughters down the centuries. Personally, the individual I feel for most in the story (Luke 15:11–32) is the fatted calf: when the soft old dad realises his son is safe, his agenda is simple: meeting, greeting and eating!

I can empathise with the fatted calf, for since I arrived at St Margaret's, Ilkley, to prepare for tomorrow's licensing, delicacies such as a Fat Rascal (a Yorkshire treat: part scone, part rock cake), two ginger cakes and 'two small fishes' (John 6:9) have appeared almost daily from Betty's, Ilkley's upper-crust tea shop and bakery. In addition, I have been given over a dozen bottles of wine. The vicarage faces on to the famous 'Ilkla Moor', but I might be in one of Ulster's six counties: Fermanagh, Armagh, Tyrone, Londonderry, Antrim and Down. Do they want me to become a 'FAT LAD', and does anyone know it's Lent? Someone has even penned a new version of *Land of Hope and Glory*:

> Land of Hope and glory;
> it's like a jubilee –
> our own dear Archbishop
> is joining us in Ilkley.

> He'll be God's faithful servant
> (and do a good job, I bet);
> preserve us in temptation, Lord –
> and deliver us from debt!

The last line makes sense, for St Margaret's still needs well over £100,000 to pay for a new parish hall rising above the ashes of the old, which was demolished a few weeks ago.

Despite all this kindness, which is most encouraging, I am reminded of a remark by the late Scottish theologian William Barclay that if we could have just one prayer for ourselves, perhaps it should be for a sense of proportion. In a few weeks' time, 'Hope hype' will have disappeared and I shall have chucked off for good the chains of high office to get back to where I once belonged – as a parish priest seeking to serve God in all those whom he sends my way. To keep things in perspective, I shall aim to do it 'thy way' – which involves first and foremost the discipline of a public and private prayer routine. I could not do better than echo the words of a hymn by George Herbert, the great clergyman-poet who died on this day in 1633:

> Teach me, my God and king,
> in all things thee to see;
> and what I do in anything
> to do it as for thee!

To Herbert, all things in our daily lives will take on new meaning if shared with God. Heaven is not just beyond the finishing post – it is also waiting to be discovered in the race we're already running.

❧ *Wednesday 2 March*
LICENSING DAY

Here beginneth the last day on which I must read Morning
Prayer in the vicarage. By convention, Anglican clergy do not
normally go into the church where they are to serve until
they have received legal authority and been given the keys.

The majestic moor just outside my door, the yellow and
purple of the daffodils and crocuses – and the kindness shown
to me already – make it more than a mere duty at 6.30 am to
say the *Te Deum*:

> We praise Thee, O God,
> we acknowledge Thee to be the Lord,
> all the Earth doth worship Thee,
> the Father everlasting …

Then it's time for tea and porridge, made with bran and
honey (in summer I usually have Weetabix or Shredded
Wheat). *Te Deum* and tea … but there'll be no tedium today,
with plenty to do before 500 people arrive at St Margaret's
tonight, eager to see 'The Three Davids'.

I am to be welcomed at the licensing by David Lee,
Archdeacon of Bradford, who shocked evangelical churchgoers in Birmingham recently by telling them God sometimes wants people to stay away from worship. 'Sin is
whenever we resist what God desires. If a person goes to
church, and God desires that they stay at home writing to
relatives they have neglected, going to church is sinful!' I trust
the number of those due to attend today's service who
develop pangs of conscience around teatime is relatively few.
The service is to be conducted by Bishop David James, who
gained several young admirers when he last visited St
Margaret's by tearing a £10 note in half at the 9.30 am

Family Service. This being Yorkshire, he had borrowed someone else's tenner!

After breakfast, I wade into the letters and e-mails. The amounts are now reasonable, but when it was announced I was resigning as Archbishop to become a parish priest, I received up to 120 letters a day – and, for a while, I was tempted to make an addition to the Lord's Prayer: 'Deliver us from e-mails!' I wasn't surprised by the pressure, having realised early on that being about the Lord's business entailed extreme busy-ness at Bishopthorpe. York's railway station is impressive, but it doesn't always seem so at 6 am when you've a meeting to attend in London. Often my day would start at 4.30 am and continue until 11 pm; most weeks I put in at least 60 hours. Perhaps the greatest strain came from being like a doctor who is on duty – constantly on call, even on holiday.

My first interviewer today, BBC *Look North* reporter Cathy Killick, appears less concerned about my views on women priests and homosexual clergy than the carpet in the vicarage kitchen, which she considers too light for a room in which food is prepared. I tell her not to be cheeky and to come back in five years' time.

The next interview is with Sarah Lewthwaite, a producer from Radio 4's religious programme *Sunday*; I keep it short by leaving to meet a friend arriving at Leeds-Bradford Airport. Back at the vicarage, family members start to arrive. After numerous cups of tea, at 6 pm I chat in church with Bishop David to the *Ilkley Gazette*, whose deadline is fast approaching, and Robert Pigott, the BBC Religious Affairs Correspondent, for Radio 4's *Today* programme. At 6.30 pm it's time for a live chat with Harry Gration, joint presenter with Christa Ackroyd of *Look North* – known locally as 'The Harry-Christa Show'. In 2002 Harry acted as compère at a celebrity auction held by St Margaret's in aid of our parish hall appeal fund. He has a harder job tonight, since our organist, Christian Spence, has pulled out most, if not all, the stops for a powerful performance of Bach's *Prelude and Fugue in C Minor*.

The service is centred round a series of promises at appropriate places in the church – for example, at the font to 'build up the Lord's household'; at the door to 'welcome friend and stranger alike'. To every question, the reply is, 'With the help of God, I will.' Apparently someone has suggested that to the question, 'Will you set time aside for prayer and reflection?' I should respond, 'I've said more prayers than you've had hot dinners!' Of course, such a boast would be sinful, but presumably also true. After all, you can make many petitions in five minutes, but we only eat one dinner per day – which in much of Yorkshire is at midday ('tea' follows work) but in posh Ilkley is usually 'on a night' (they don't say THAT here, of course) – often preceded by a G and T, sherry or cocktail.

David Lee does not overdo the welcoming, and Bishop David's sermon on humility is also a sensible length. He is upbeat about a current 'vocations epidemic' in the Diocese, and adds that many Christians, both lay and ordained, are making great sacrifices for their faith. David makes some good points, but all the while I can't help thinking, 'He's giving the care of this parish to me, just as I entrusted Bradford Diocese to him nearly three years ago; God does indeed move in a mysterious way!' The service is an emotionally charged occasion, and I feel enfolded in prayer and love – everyone seems so buoyant!

Instead of shaking hands with people leaving the church, I go straight to the Clarke-Foley Centre in Cunliffe Road, where I manage to speak with nearly everyone during the buffet reception. While most people are finishing their meal, I head for the bar to chat with the men serving drinks, most of whom are now tucking into burgers and chips. A plate of chips is handed to Trevor Hearnshaw, once an active church member, who now suffers from Alzheimer's Disease. It somehow feels special to share some of his chips: it may be Lent, but Jesus teaches us that the duties of love always come before outward religious observations.

Towards the end of the evening there are speeches of welcome, most notably by Barbara France, who with her churchwarden colleague John Sunderland had interviewed me for the vacancy. Barbara, also the church treasurer, has been reflecting on 'My Favourite Things' from *The Sound of Music*. She says:

> I realised that raindrops on roses and whiskers on kittens were not included on my list of favourite things. Number one was returning from holiday, going into St Margaret's, feeling warm and realising I had come home.

My thoughts turn to St Margaret's marvellous choir (which I have heard several times in recent years), the church's faithful observance of the Christian seasons, its devotion to the Reserved Sacrament, and the sense of God's peace in the building, so often commented on by visitors.

I cannot help but add: 'I know how you feel – I have come home too.'

❧ *Thursday 3 March*

> And be not like their fathers, a stiff-necked and uncontrolled generation; a generation whose heart was hard, whose spirit was not true to God.
>
> (Psalm 78:8, *The Bible in Basic English*)

Everyone is 'stiff-necked' at times in falling short of how God would have us live; Christians go to church to enable God's love to 'bridge the gap' between him and them so it can flow out into his world.

However, in a purely physical way, maybe one might expect a member of my new flock to suffer stiffness above the shoulders. Early in the 1980s, professional artist Graeme Willson spent two years working on a 24 x 8 ft painting now on the ceiling of St Cuthbert's Chapel in York Minster. This increased his admiration of Michelangelo, who took four years (1508–12) to re-paint the ceiling of the Sistine Chapel. In fact, for most of the time Graeme laboured on his painting, it was vertical – in St Martin's, Chapel Allerton, Leeds. It only became horizontal while he was applying the finishing touches. 'At no point was I on my back – I simply stood and leaned back,' he says. 'I'm sorry to disappoint everyone who knows about Michelangelo, but I have had absolutely no neck pain since completing the painting.'

In 1990 Graeme created an even bigger mural, measuring 32 x 30ft, on a building adjacent to the Corn Exchange in Leeds. *Cornucopia* includes almost everything corny but jokes – such as Victorian corn-traders, a cherub bearing a basket of rolls, and Ceres, the Roman corn goddess. The mural produces mixed reactions, but it certainly impressed Morrisons, the Northern supermarket giant, who commissioned Graeme to create murals and stained glass at their stores in Glasgow, Darlington, Manchester, Crewe, Bradford, Sheffield and Norwich.

As I mentioned earlier, in April 2004 I had visited St Margaret's to dedicate Graeme's painting *The Madonna of the Moors*. In the painting Mary is presenting Jesus to us, the onlookers, while the Baptiser holds a lamb and a rough wooden cross – a reference to his prophetic remark: 'Here is the Lamb of God who takes away the sin of the world!' (John 1:29). This memorable painting is attracting visitors from a wide area. More reasons to worship at the moor church!

❧ *Friday 4 March*

After the excitement of the licensing, I came back to earth with a bump last night at a meeting at Christ Church, Skipton, where assessors explained how the share which each parish pays to the Diocese is fixed. Hardly riveting stuff, but in the end it's 'brass' that keeps the show on the road. Not one person among the 75 present whinged about the 'unfairness' of their particular parish's share. I think I shall like it around here!

Today, for one day only, St Margaret's Playtime becomes the *Funday Times*, when *Sunday Times* Royal/Religion writer Christopher Morgan comes to interview me. He wants a flavour of our parish life, and what better than the organised chaos of our parents-and-toddlers playgroup? Life was easier when St Margaret's Playtime met in the old parish hall; since it was demolished, all the equipment has had to be stowed at the back of the church, along with items including a portable stage for musical performances.

Two dads join in the nursery rhymes and are among the 40-strong audience as a puppet show takes place on the font, followed by an enthusiastic rendering of 'Incy Wincy Spider'. In the confusion I can't make out if Christopher is joining in, but it wouldn't be beneath his dignity to do so. A young mum newly arrived from the south is obviously enjoying herself, and the men confess to being at home among all the ladies.

The Church is at its best when serving people 'where they are' without bashing them with propaganda. If those attending Playtime feel welcome, some may start wondering what motivates the helpers to give up their Friday mornings week after week. Despite the occasional minor crisis, they keep coming back – like Robert the Bruce after he saw that spider persevering.

I have enjoyed my first experience of St Margaret's

Playtime, and I hope the *Sunday Times* man has, too. Maybe we should tell the story of his visit on our website.

✤ *Saturday 5 March*

A day to catch my breath and finish off the main sermon for tomorrow. As it's my first Sunday, I am also preaching at the other two morning services, but those talks can be off the cuff. Talking of which, before and after lunch I wash my shirts and sheets. Brother Lawrence, the saintly author of *The Practice of the Presence of God*, advised anyone seeking a deepened spiritual awareness to pray while doing domestic chores. I usually curse!

In the evening Cantores Olicanae, an Ilkley choir who perform regularly in St Margaret's, present Bach's *St John Passion*. It's a powerful and moving work with some magnificent chorales. Tomorrow will be busy, so I don't stop to chat afterwards and am in bed by 10.30 pm.

✤ *Sunday 6 March 2005*

After meeting the regulars who attend the 8 am service, I hurry out to buy the *Sunday Times*. You can always trust the Lord, but journalists ... Fortunately, Christopher Morgan has produced quite a kind article with perhaps only a shade too much stress on my wheelie-bin:

> For 10 years, his every need was catered for in his personal grace-and-favour palace. This weekend, David Hope, the former Archbishop of York and the second most powerful man in the Church of England, was to be found clattering a black [dark green, actually] wheelie bin across the pavement in front of a modest Yorkshire vicarage.
>
> 'I put it out late last night,' he said cheerily. Showing

Christian concern, he also pushed his neighbours' bin back to their home ...

Maybe the wheelie-bin should feature in a sermon on Mark 4:22 ('For there is nothing hidden, except to be disclosed ...')? Donovan's 1965 album *What's Bin Did and What's Bin Hid* could be cited – except on collection-day, bins in genteel Ilkley are invariably 'outa sight'! My wheelie could even cast light on Ezekiel's vision of the 'wheels within wheels':

> As I looked at the living creatures, I saw a wheel on the earth beside the living creatures, one for each of the four of them. As for the appearance of the wheels and their construction: their appearance was like the gleaming of beryl; and the four had the same form, their construction being something like a wheel within a wheel.
>
> (Ezekiel 1:15–16)

There are 60–70 children and adults at the 9.30 am half-hour Family Service, a growth point for St Margaret's introduced by my predecessor, Fr Richard Hoyal, now Priest-in-Charge of All Saints, Clifton, and All Hallows, Easton, Bristol. It's a relaxed, informal occasion, and parents needn't worry if their brood rush around, scream or are sick – they won't be the only ones! It's a far cry from my childhood at Wakefield, where you had to sit quietly under the cathedral pews and, if you didn't, there was a dragon who would slap your legs – we really were kept down in those days! As today is Mothering Sunday, I show everyone a copy of a teapot given by Josiah Wedgewood to John Wesley, which was presented to me as Bishop of London by the Minister of Wesley's Chapel. On it is written:

> We thank Thee, Lord, for this our food,
> but more because of Jesus' love.

A joke or funny story always helps to break the ice when meeting people, so I begin the sermon at the 10.30 am Solemn Eucharist with a reference to Ruth – not the husband of Boaz mentioned in the Old Testament book of Ruth, but Ruth Gledhill, religious correspondent of *The Times*. The other day I made the mistake of telling her that I enjoy *Car Magazine* and *Railway Enthusiast*, and since her article appeared I've been deluged with unsolicited mail about both forms of transport. I don't know how Ruth imagines I can 'now indulge to the full' my interests in cars and trains in a town with so many nursing homes to visit, just for a start. Certainly until Easter, the demands of learning about my new parish will postpone my plan to take Mondays off. My sermon's theme concerns the healing of a man blind from birth (John 9). A handful of those present may remember my point that to the Evangelist the water used by Jesus in the healing is a symbol of the Holy Spirit's work through baptism, but I suspect that within a week most will only retain my anecdote about the visiting journalist!

During coffee after the service I decide not to try too hard to remember the names of everyone I've met – that will come before long. Most people are still excited about my arrival; I shall be glad when all that has worn off and I'm just another member of the clergy team. I can't help noticing that since I arrived no one has mentioned a single issue discussed at the General Synod the other week – it makes one wonder how relevant such gatherings are to the life of the Church at parish level.

My final engagement of the day is a short evening service at Abbeyfield Ilkley Grove House, a care centre for old people which opened a year ago. About 25 residents are present, and I am relieved to discover they are not bothered either way about my being there!

❧ *Monday 7 March*

Much of the day is spent in my office, preparing for the parish Annual General Meeting at 7.45 pm. AGMs are notorious for rows, and as Archbishop I occasionally received complaints from churches about procedures supposedly not being followed, elections being rigged, and people calling each other names.

How often, I wonder, do those showing at best a lack of charity to their fellow-Christians consider the Lord's words:

> 'By this everyone will know that you are my disciples, if you have love for one another' (John 13:35)?

The hard-hitting First Letter of John spells out in no uncertain terms what it means to be uncharitable:

> We know that we have passed from death to life because we love one another. Whoever does not love abides in death. (1 John 3:14)

Fortunately, my first few days at St Margaret's have shown me how united this church is – a pattern for the wider Church. John Baggaley, a new churchwarden, reported in the parish magazine that to maintain good relationships during the interregnum (the period between priests), the PCC had suggested to the patrons (the Community of the Resurrection) that on balance it would be 'inappropriate' for a woman to work in this particular church. There was not one objection from those in favour of women priests – and no back-biting, I gather.

People are kind to me at the AGM, but do I detect a challenge to their Christian charity? For moving around the church with her microphone again – for the third time? – is Sarah Lewthwaite, the Radio 4 producer, whose persistence provokes some mild grumbling afterwards about her 'intru-siveness'. Having been besieged by the media for many months, I shall be relieved when life returns to normal. At one stage I thought the press were going to request photos not only of the packing cases but also their contents!

❧ *Tuesday 8 March*

Today there's a chapter meeting at Farnley, near Otley, for the clergy of the Otley Deanery, which includes Ilkley. We are discussing a proposal to reduce our numbers by two before 2007, and are expected to suggest where the cuts should be made. It's a bit like asking a group of turkeys who wants to go to a Christmas dinner.

Some people think the proposal is not radical enough: with an increasing role for the laity in worship and non-stipendiary (unpaid) ministers, even fewer full-time clergy might be need-ed. Others argue that since the Otley Deanery contributes most money to Bradford Diocese, it should be spared any cuts.

The talk is tedious and in circles. Several of those present feel the Diocese has no clear strategy over the issue and is not giving enough leadership if it has. It's a relief to be back at the vicarage, where Assistant Priest Fr Alan Brown arrives at 7.30 pm for an informal dedication of the house and blessing on my time here. He walks around, sprinkling holy water in each room. Alan is an Oblate of the Community of the Resurrection at Mirfield, near Wakefield – someone dedicated to the monastic life but not professed. Having worked as a nurse and in Health Service administration, Alan is now Senior Lecturer in the School of Healthcare at Leeds University. He was ordained deacon in 1995 and priest in 1996. He's been a 'wandering star' in the Diocese, but returned to St Margaret's during the interregnum which followed Fr Richard's departure for Bristol.

❧ *Wednesday 9 March*

It's that woman again – Sarah Lewthwaite, the Radio 4 producer, has persuaded me to be interviewed walking on Ilkley
Moor. At first I wonder why this is necessary for radio, but
then I reflect that she must want to capture the sound of
bleating sheep in the background.

After an ecumenical lunch with clergy colleagues at
Methodist minister Chris Sharp's home, I call on Val Roberts,
who leads an inter-denominational rosary group at her home
opposite Tesco. I am reminded of the story of an elderly Irish
Catholic woman who goes to the confessional and reads out:

> ½lb cheese
> bananas
> potatoes
> carrots
> rice pudding
> cat food

'What's this?' asks the puzzled priest.

'Holy Mary and all the Saints,' is the reply, 'I must have left
my sins in Tesco!' Like some of the clergymen I know, the old
ones are the best!

It's the sick list, not the sin list, that I've come to talk about
with Val, because we agree it has grown too long. We decide
that in future only the names of the acutely ill will appear on
the pew-sheet handed out on Sundays; the other names will
be put on the prayer desk in front of the Lady Chapel.

I'm often asked how prayer works – if at all. Perhaps it is by
breaking down the barriers of space and time: through it, we
are drawn more fully into God's will and purposes for us and
those for whom we are praying. We often have half a mind to
tell God what 'to do', as though we know best. But what we

need to do is to surrender that person or persons ('letting go, letting God') to absolute Love, whose purposes in life and death are always accomplished for us and the entire world. Even when our expectations of God don't seem to be fulfilled, he is still working in ways we don't yet understand but shall do some day.

❧ *Thursday 10 March*

At last – a day off, walking alone in the Dales. When Jesus tried to 'get away from it all', someone invariably joined in.

❧ *Friday 11 March*

After Playtime I take Holy Communion to a sick parishioner at Airedale General Hospital, near Keighley. Later I'm at the official opening of Abbeyfield Ilkley Grove House, which is greatly improving the quality of life of those who live there or attend during the day. The young are often seen as central to the Church's mission, but to the Lord the elderly are just as important. As St Augustine remarked: 'God loves each one of us as if there was only one of us to love.'

❧ *Saturday 12 March*

The only drawback to living above Ilkley, a mere stone's throw from the moor, is the sheep which descend like Byron's wolf on the fold, somehow negotiate the cattle-grid and head straight for the vicarage garden, where the grass is always greener. Occasionally, they even go into St Margaret's, but unfortunately any offerings they make are not yet eligible for Gift Aid.

St Francis of Assisi would no doubt smile benignly at these ram-raids and non-ewe behaviour. But what I need is Ollie the Collie, a super sheep-gatherer created for young readers by Leslie Simpson, founder of the British Society of Painters, who persuaded me to open their spring exhibition at the Winter Garden today. Leslie is an amazing, unassuming man who started painting aged five, has never had a lesson and now, aged 75, has discovered his métier in Ollie and his Whimsicollie friends.

Ollie, based on Leslie's youngest border collie, Meg, is a brainy problem-solving sheepdog ('A dog Poirot,' says Leslie). Eight border collies, including Leslie's three (great friends of his cat Lottie) joined in (or rather caused!) the excitement when *The Adventures of Ollie the Collie*, by Leslie and London journalist Russell Forgham, was launched at The Grove Bookshop last month. There was a limited first edition of 500 signed copies, and I am the proud owner of number 270!

Previous art show openers have included a host of TV soap celebrities, and when *Emmerdale* star Cleveland Campbell was delayed at the opening of the related British Watercolour Society exhibition last December, Leslie spotted Richard ('Mr Countdown') Whiteley, who lives near Ilkley, passing by on his way to a wedding and roped him in instead! 'Someone was working on our side,' says Leslie.

Today Leslie's son Nigel, who owns a wedding car hire business, offers to chauffeur me downhill to the Winter Garden in his white Rolls Royce. I politely decline the offer, saying I am in the business of taking weddings, not being on the receiving end, and prefer to walk!

Afterwards, Leslie and his wife Margaret kindly take me to La Sila Ristorante for a delicious lunch of pizza, pollo crema and cappuccino. Margaret, like me, grew up in Wakefield, so we have a lot to chat about and I'm nearly half-way to Paradise. And to think I could still be at Bishopthorpe Palace, preparing for the next General Synod meeting ...

❧ *Sunday 13 March*
PASSION SUNDAY

Today all the crosses in church are draped in purple, the colour of the robe which the soldiers put on Jesus before they beat him up. The sombre mood in St Margaret's draws everyone more closely into the mystery of the Passion.

My Sundays here are going to be full. Today I am up at 6.05 am for the 8 am service and not back home until 1 pm. After lunch I read the papers, stroll on Ilkley Moor and at 4 pm start preparing for next week. I'm back in church at 5.30 pm for Evensong, and don't leave until 8 pm.

❧ *Tuesday 15 March*

Ilkley is such a pleasant place to be – close to Leeds and Bradford, but surrounded by beautiful countryside – that it's ideal for retirement, and several retired priests regularly assist at our services. Today two of them visit to exchange ideas. They are obviously a blessing, but there are limits on what they can do – one of them doesn't go out at night and several take quite a lot of time off, and of course there are little matters like arrangements for collecting keys to consider.

It will be a great help when Lay Reader Garth Kellett is ordained deacon in June, since he will have a regular routine of duties.

❧ *Wednesday 16 March*

When it comes to food, I'm not a disciple of the health police. They can keep their lettuce leaves – I'd rather resemble a rabbi than a rabbit! So at lunchtime I'm in the kitchen, looking forward to a wholesome meal of baked beans, fried eggs and bacon (done in olive oil, I stress!) following a

Standing Committee meeting dealing with 'nitty-gritty' matters about church fabric. Everything is coming together nicely, when Baptist minister Stuart Jenkins rings the doorbell saying he is ready to take me to 'the meeting'. I have completely forgotten the Ilkley Clergy's ecumenical prayer-lunch!

I say, 'Good gracious', but don't own up to having been about to eat. I ask Stuart to wait a minute, charge into the kitchen like a man possessed, turn off the gas and, with a sigh, put my delicious lunch into the cooker out of sight.

Off we go to All Saints' vicarage, where Paul Tudge has forgotten *he* is hosting the lunch and is raiding the larder for tins of Tesco soup. It proves a 'scratch' lunch – Paul scratches together anything he can find! The clergy begin praying 'as the Spirit moves them'. Paul gives thanks for 'a time of quiet amid the rush', then leaps up to stir the soup. He sits down for more quiet, then bounces up again like the man lame from birth cured by Peter and John (Acts 3:1–10). Quiet descends again – until a tiny Tudge trudges into the room. Of your charity, pray excuse Paul and me for our forgetfulness. After all, we clergy have a lot on our plates – even if it's not always eggs, bacon and beanz!

ꙮ *Thursday 17 March*

It's that man again – Leslie ('Ollie the Collie') Simpson. St Margaret's has just commissioned a painting from him recalling probably the most bizarre event in the church's history.

On 16 August 2002, the Silver Jubilee of Elvis Presley's death, an Elvis impersonation competition was held at St Margaret's to raise funds for the parish hall appeal and a cancer research appeal led by the Bradford *Telegraph and Argus*. About 10 Elvis fanatics wiggled their pelvises, the winner being an 11-year-old girl, Jessica Meehan, from Bradford.

The event was beset by problems, especially when the

backing band backed out, and Fr Richard Hoyal was on the brink of crying in the chapel until big-hearted Elvis impersonator Peter Henderson, from Leeds, stepped in with his karaoke equipment – no doubt to the relief of his neighbours!

Q: 'And who is my neighbour?' (Luke 10:29)
A: They include people who serenade you after a hard day at the office with an enthusiastic rendering of 'Are You Lonesome Tonight?'

For months after the event Fr Richard told people that when he died, the word 'Elvis' would surely be found engraved on his heart! On 29 June at All Saints, Clifton, Richard is due to celebrate 25 years in the priesthood. To mark the anniversary, we have asked Leslie to depict a guitar-playing collie wearing a clerical collar, with the caption, 'You Ain't Nothin' But a Hound Dog-Collar'. Richard deserves this unexpected 'treat' – he laid the foundations of the goodwill which I am benefiting from and there's evidence of his fine pastoral work all over Ilkley.

NB If you are lonesome tonight, we know some friendly Elvis impersonators who, I'm sure, would be pleased for you to join them elsewhere. *This* town has been all shook up enough for quite a while – certainly until 2027.

❧ *Friday 18 March*

Bishop David James calls for an hour this afternoon to see how I am settling in. It's thoughtful of him – as Bishop of Wakefield, I visited new clergy when I had the time. Bishops have many duties both inside and outside the Church, but to me their biggest responsibility is towards their biggest asset – the clergy, who deserve support both before and after they begin their ministry.

❧ Saturday 19 March

Those who sometimes feel they play an insignificant role in the life and witness of the Church can take heart from the example of St Joseph, husband of the Virgin Mary, whose feast day we celebrate today. He was behind the scenes in the original nativity play, but what an important part this enabler had – in saving Mary and Jesus from King Herod, and later providing a stable home environment in which the lad's potential could develop. Without today's enablers (people like you and your friends?) many Christians who in due course receive good reviews wouldn't have progressed beyond the dress rehearsal!

❧ Sunday 20 March

PALM SUNDAY

Today we mark the day on which Jerusalem went wild with excitement as Jesus entered it in triumph on a donkey.

Here at St Margaret's the children at our Family Service are pretty enthusiastic about a model donkey borrowed from Otley Deanery, while the adults are impressed by a knitted version of the Last Supper made by parishioner Pat Patterson, who has spent virtually all of Lent creating Jesus and the Twelve behind a table with plates of white (knitted!) bread and cups of red (knitted!) wine. As in many paintings of the event, John is clean-shaven but everyone else is bearded.

The Palm Sunday processions are not just reminders of a past historical event. In Jesus, the world of space and time was invaded by eternity, enabling the victory of the Cross to flow out into every place and time – as the lawyers would say, 'It was a single act with continuing consequences.' In a mysterious way, when we re-enact the events of the Passion in faith,

Christ discloses himself as alive today and catches us up into the transforming power of his risen life. At times in our lives we may all feel like Christ in Gethsemane – forsaken by God – but through the events of Holy Week Christ assures us of his never-ending love for us, whatever our circumstances. We may stray very far from him; he will never leave us.

❧ *Monday 21 March*

> Vanity of vanities, says the Teacher; all is vanity.
> (Ecclesiastes 12:8)

I ought to look my best in Holy Week. I know the barber can't do much in my case, and I don't suppose even seeking the intercession of St Jude, the Patron Saint of Lost Causes, would help my 'lot' – or little, rather – but I tell myself it is important to be out and about meeting all sorts of people, including hairdressers. Today there's a chance to talk about holidays, rather than holy days.

Back at the vicarage I spend some time with parishioner Teresa Cannell, who designs our Sunday news and service sheets. Teresa, who grew up in Romford, is a lively and capable 'Essex lady'. Before her retirement, she was a secretary with a publishing company and later a firm of shipbrokers.

This will be a busy week, with Evening Mass today, tomorrow and on Wednesday in addition to the important four days starting on Thursday.

❧ *Tuesday 22 March*

I have developed a terrible infection under the nail in the fourth finger of my right hand. Some pious people in my position might say, 'This will help me to reflect better on Christ's sufferings', but all I can say is, 'Ouch!' My quack has the nerve to ask, 'Do you bite your nails?', to which I respond, 'Certainly not!' He puts me on a course of wretched antibiotics for 10 days.

A site meeting with the architect and others involved with the building of the new parish hall concentrates my mind for a while, as does hearing several pre-Easter confessions. Later I busy myself with preparations for the Maundy Thursday and Easter Day services.

ॐ *Wednesday 23 March*

The busiest four days of the year are nearly upon us, so I try to use today well by 'resting in God' during the daily Offices at 7.45 am and 6 pm. I am normally in church every morning by 7 am in search of the still centre which puts into context everything else that may happen during the next 24 hours. As many in the Jewish, Christian and Muslim traditions have found, life develops a rhythm if the new day is valued as a gift and the evening is a time for 'giving back' to the Almighty those people and situations with which we have been involved.

ॐ *Thursday 24 March*
MAUNDY THURSDAY

It is nearly midnight, the hour at which, according to tradition, Jesus was arrested. Here in St Margaret's, the candles and cloths have been removed from the altar and the sanctuary is empty, reflecting the desolation of the Lord, abandoned even by his closest friends soon after the Last Supper. But in the Lady Chapel candles burn on and a vase of lilies, representing the Gethsemane garden, stands near the aumbrey [small cupboard] containing the Host who shares with us at each Holy Communion his victory over sin and death.

Groups of parishioners have stayed on after the 8 pm Eucharist or come back, keen to 'stay awake' with Jesus. It is still (so still!) in the Lady Chapel; the stillness is like the peace which descends after Midnight Mass on Christmas Eve.

Earlier, along with Fr Alan Brown and retired Canon Bernard Gribbin, I have imitated Jesus by washing the feet of a representative group of church members. The Epistle was from 1 Corinthians 11, the earliest account of the Last Supper:

> For as often as you eat this bread and drink the cup, you proclaim the Lord's death until he comes.

As we wait on God, the power operating through events long past breaks into the present via the consecrated bread and wine.

To many people, God is either the chairman of the interview panel or a disinterested spectator viewing from a distance the suffering of the world. But the mystery of Jesus is that, as God Incarnate ('in flesh'), he is a suffering servant, the beyond-in-the-midst; the bread and wine of Holy Communion symbolise that, like us, he was 'flesh and blood'. At the same time, the Eucharist also celebrates the presence of the risen and glorified Christ, sacramentally present in our midst.

As perfect man, he is a bridge between God and humanity – the only human good enough to bridge the gulf between God and us, divided from God and others by self-centredness. The victory of love over self-will won on Calvary is channelled through the Body and Blood – making every Eucharist a mini-Easter. This love is stronger than anything we might have to go through, such as loneliness, redundancy, illness and bereavement.

❧ *Friday 25 March*
GOOD FRIDAY

It is drizzling, and some of those arriving at All Saints in Skipton Road have brought their brollies for the procession of witness arranged by Churches Together in Ilkley. A stream of cars is heading along the A65 between Kendal and Leeds – 'Is it nothing to you, all you who pass by?'

After a reading and hymn outside the church at 11.15 am, worshippers follow the Revd Brian Gregory, vicar of St John's, Ben Rhydding, Ilkley, who for the past 12 years has carried a home-made cross around Ilkley centre on this day.

We pause in the town square in front of La Sila Restorante, Kids Unlimited and The Candy Box. Behind us, Asquiths the greengrocers are selling daffodils, tulips, pansies and an occasional Flowerpot Man (£4.99) on their forecourt. Brian leads us across two zebra crossings to the Post Office and then along Ilkley's main street, The Grove, where a larger cross will be fixed throughout Eastertide between Dacre, Son and Hartley, estate agents, and the Abbey National.

This year around 150 people are on the procession of witness – more than normal because St Margaret's have rearranged the services to enable our people to attend. Some of the hymns are rather high for baritones and basses (St Margaret's has a reputation for being 'high'!) but we do our best, especially Lay Reader Garth Kellett, who has possibly the deepest voice in Ilkley!

Outside Christchurch, the reading is from Psalm 22:20:

> Deliver my soul from the sword,
> my life from the power of the dog!

A dog is among the procession which ends at the bandstand on The Grove, but it's only a friendly labrador – and in any case is on a strong lead! In a short talk, I remind everyone that in a world where many are poor, hungry and affected by AIDS and other diseases, Jesus' acceptance of suffering on the Cross is a divine challenge to our comfort and complacency – we are called to reach out in service locally and do what we can to relieve suffering worldwide.

At 2 pm, back in St Margaret's, there is again deep silence as Fr Alan Brown carries a small, veiled cross up the nave aisle to a position under the rood screen where Christ is depicted hanging on a larger cross dominating the church. To the response, 'Come and worship', three times Alan intones:

> 'This is the wood of the cross on which hung the Saviour of the world.'

Parishioners kneel one by one before the Maker of both tiny acorn and giant California Redwoods, who was laid in a wooden manger, worked with wood as a joiner and ended his life nailed to a plank. As an Orthodox hymn for Good Friday puts it:

> Today he who hung the earth upon the waters is hung upon the Cross.

In the face of such a deep mystery, we leave the church startled again into silence.

❧ *Saturday 26 March*
HOLY SATURDAY

After the quiet contemplation of Good Friday, church members spring into activity to get St Margaret's ready for the greatest festival of all tomorrow. The women are busy arranging flowers, while the men are involved in heavy lifting. Fr Alan Brown and I meet the servers in a rehearsal for the evening Easter Vigil.

No one knows the time of Jesus' Resurrection, but there is a keen sense of anticipation at 7.30 pm as the Vigil begins in darkness. Into this blackness comes God's declaration, 'Let there be light' (Genesis 1:3). Soon afterwards the Paschal Candle is lit in honour of the Risen Christ – Light of the World.

✤ Sunday 27 March
EASTER DAY

Very early in the morning on the first day of the week, at sunrise, Mary of Magdala, Mary the mother of James, and Salome brought spices to the tomb to anoint the body of Jesus. You and I are so familiar with what the Church believes happened next that we can take this for granted. Perhaps we should try to put ourselves in those women's sandals. The Resurrection of Jesus came as such a shock to them that Mark, writer of the earliest Gospel, records that they ran from the tomb not with joy, but with terror (Mark 16:1–8).

Very early today (6.15 am – it would have been 5.15 am yesterday), about 50 Christians and four dogs begin gathering at the Cow and Calf Rocks above Ilkley for an ecumenical Sunrise ('Son-Rise') service.

Geza Vermes, Professor Emeritus of Jewish Studies at Oxford University, has recently calculated the date of Jesus' death as falling on 7 April in AD 30. Assuming this is correct, and deducting 11 days to allow for the adjustment to the Gregorian calendar, I calculate that the sun has risen 721,330 times over Ilkley Moor from the Crucifixion until today. The moor consists of millstone grit from the Upper Carboniferous period and is over 300 million years old. But, as Hugh remembers Fr Richard Hoyal saying once in a sermon on Christmas Eve, 'Before the dinosaurs were, the Word already was.' Psalm 90 hints at something still more wonderful – that the Love which has existed from eternity has always been concerned about humanity, including, today, *you and me*:

> Lord, you have been our dwelling-place
> in all generations.
> Before the mountains were brought forth,
> or ever you had formed the earth and the world,
> from everlasting to everlasting you are God …

At 6.34 am, Methodist minister the Revd Chris Sharp shouts out the traditional Easter acclamation: 'Alleluia! Christ is risen!', to which the joyful response is: 'He is risen indeed. Alleluia!' Led by Cyril Taylor (71), a trumpeter with Guiseley Brass Band, the *al fresco* congregation sends a 'wake up' song down towards the town. It's not yet fully light, so Cyril plays by torchlight. After prayers, the worshippers affirm their faith in 'our God loving us to death … embracing us to eternity'. Brian Gregory reads the earliest account of the Resurrection (Mark 16:1–8). At 6.50 am the words of 'Thine be the glory, risen, conquering Son' drift through the mist. A few rolls are broken and shared, and everyone receives a chocolate mini-egg. By 7 am the last of the cars is setting off on the steep descent into Ilkley. At 7.05 am Brian is busy fastening daffodils to the cross on The Grove.

I enjoy opening up the church in good time for the 8 am service, which enables me to sit in silence for a while before all Heaven breaks loose! Fr Alan Brown brings some decent-sized chocolate eggs for the children attending the 9.30 am Family Mass, and at 10.30 am, in honour of the day, I am in my bishop's gear of robe, mitre and staff. After the austerity of

Lent and Passiontide, an army of volunteers has been at work and the church is a mass of candles and flowers. The Easter Garden beneath the pulpit, which includes heather from Ilkley Moor, is magnificent!

Anyone who reads the accounts of the Easter event by the four Evangelists is bound to be struck by the differences in their recording of Christ's Resurrection appearances. In today's sermon I say that while some have found this a hindrance to belief, to me it fits our actual human experience. Along with others, I once witnessed a road accident. From the statements given to the police it was evident that the only clear fact on which everyone agreed was that the accident had involved a bus and a car. Similarly, the accounts of the Resurrection appearances may differ, yet the gospel writers were unanimous about the heart of the matter – the tomb was empty and Jesus Christ was alive! Yet the Resurrection is not simply something which happened in or around AD 30. Here today at this communion rail Jesus Christ stands before us as he did in the garden. Unseen, but not unknown, he speaks his word of peace and sends us out into a troubled world with the good news for all of his risen life – 'Do not be afraid; I am the first and the last, and the living one. I was dead, and see, I am alive for ever and ever ...' (Revelation 1:17–18).

❧ Monday 28 March

I breathe a sigh of relief at having got Easter Day over (although Eastertide will be with us until Ascension Day on 5 May).

I hope that doesn't sound too disrespectful. It has been hectic since I started here only 26 days ago, with the media scrum preceding the licensing, the event itself and then the build-up to Holy Week (which involved much preparation for the services) and the non-stop nature of the past four days.

Today is a day of freedom beginning with a quiet Low Mass. I spend some time in town and more on the moor, thankful not to have to think of just one more thing!

❧ *Thursday 31 March*

Rather an unusual item in the post this morning from the Department of Constitutional Affairs. It's a letter to The Lord Hope of Thornes (where I grew up in Wakefield) from Alex Allan, Clerk of the Crown in Chancery.

It says:

> The Lord Chancellor has asked me to let you know that the preliminary formalities relating to your peerage are now complete. The Letters Patent of Creation were sealed this morning and you should now sign formal documents in your new style. Notice of your elevation [I am still 5 ft 10 ins tall] has been sent to both the London and Edinburgh Gazettes for publication as soon as possible.

Then there's a trickier bit:

> I have also been asked to let you know that the Register of Lords' Interests will be writing to you separately with information regarding the Register of Interests.

I suppose I could put down 'cars and railways'. This is all a bit crazy, but the letter is not an early April Fool's joke – joining the House of Lords is customary for retiring archbishops. I won't need a new Coat of Arms, as I have one, inscribed *Spe Gaudientes* ('rejoicing in hope'), from my time as Bishop of London. The ceremony is due to take place on 21 June.

April

✣ Saturday 2 April

Six days after St Peter's confession of faith at Caesarea Philippi
– 'You are the Messiah, the Son of the living God' (Matthew
16:17) – Peter and two other leading disciples glimpsed the
glory of Jesus' divinity in the Transfiguration (Matthew
17:1–8), a vision which strengthened the Lord for his Passion.
Today, six days after the Church's Easter confession, Pope John
Paul II has entered the glory of Christ's Resurrection victory
– after years of personal suffering.

In 2000 I met the Pope at the Vatican, along with the then
President of the Methodist Conference, Dr Stuart Burgess,
and the Rt Revd John Crowley, Roman Catholic Bishop
of Middlesbrough. Although the Pope was suffering from
Parkinson's Disease, his eyes were penetrating as well as welcoming. He was gratified by the trust developing between the
churches, reminding us of Christ's prayer that '[Christians]
may be one' (John 17:11). Afterwards, the Holy Father gave
each of us a pectoral cross, which I wear occasionally with
pride and thanksgiving. He was slightly unsteady, and grasped
my hand as if he did not want to let go.

Meetings of such intensity are rare. But even in huge
crowds there was the same sense of a deeply personal and
spiritual encounter with a true man of God. And it is remarkable that people of all faiths and none have developed respect
– even affection – for him, despite disagreeing with some of
his teaching.

Already there is talk is of 'John Paul the Great'. Yet as the

Pope would remind us, the Gospels stress that any greatness comes only from recognising one's total dependence on Jesus Christ – Christ's strength in our weakness. St Irenaeus once remarked, 'The glory of God is a human person fully alive.' I am glad that Pope John Paul has been so alive in God's love and grace.

St Margaret's is packed this evening for a concert of sacred and secular music by the Steeton Male Voice Choir. The evening is organised by several members of the Family Service, whose hard work pays off – the choir are in good form, there's coffee or wine in the interval, and more than £1,000 is raised for the new parish hall appeal. Only £125,000 or so to go now!

✣ *Sunday 3 April*

After the high point of Easter Sunday, we come down to earth with a bump on 'Low Sunday'. But since every Sunday is a mini-Easter, we must travel on in faith, even if our feelings are less intense – just as newly-weds have to, once the honeymoon is over!

During the notices, I tell the congregation that during the next fortnight they will be asked to fill in forms which will be used to help in working out the share which St Margaret's pays to the Diocese. 'It is important that we do so,' I point out, 'or others will do it for us – possibly in a more optimistic way.'

✣ *Monday 4 April*

I can cook for myself, but it's a pleasure to welcome my cleaner, Ann Ashe, for the first time. While she is here, Audrey Waterhouse, a leading light in the Mothers' Union, comes to discuss dates and their programme with me. After lunch, there's a phone call from Arthur Roche, the Roman Catholic

Bishop of Leeds, who invites me to give an address in honour of Pope John Paul II during Vespers at St Anne's Cathedral, Leeds, on Wednesday. The evening is to be as ecumenical as possible in tribute to the Pope's inter-denominational – indeed inter-faith – outreach.

Tonight we have an evening Mass for the Annunciation, which marks the occasion when the Angel Gabriel told the Virgin Mary she would give birth to Jesus (Luke 1:26–38). We're only eight days into the 40 days of Eastertide, but already have one eye on Christmas. The Church is often accused of lagging behind the secular world, but at least in this respect we're streets ahead of even the most proactive retailer.

♣ *Tuesday 5 April*

An enjoyable chat with Ian Rigarlsford, a charity worker living in Burley-in-Wharfedale, and his fiancée Katie Turner, of this parish, whose marriage I am to conduct on 21 May. I haven't officiated at a wedding for at least five years, so I may be almost as nervous as the couple are. Katie's mother is here tonight to keep us in order. Such meetings are important points of contact for the clergy with people who are not among our 'regulars' but have obvious instincts for faith.

♣ *Wednesday 6 April*

St Anne's Cathedral is packed as I pay tribute to Pope John Paul II during Vespers. I recall how bright and alive the Holy Father was when I met him in 2000, despite the onset of Parkinson's. He seemed to have Christ's gift of making each person in his presence feel they were uniquely special for him at that moment. In addition to his many gifts, he was a voice with politicians for people with nothing and no voice.

I am positioned in the cathedral between Bishop Roche

and David Konstant, Emeritus Bishop of Leeds. In such
company you can't keep looking at your watch, but several of
the speakers go on perhaps a shade too much. I'm aware time
is hurrying on and I'm in danger of missing the train back to
Ilkley. Once we're in the vestry, I simply flee from the
cathedral. Moments later I am drenched by a huge cloudburst
('... [God] sends rain on the righteous and on the unright-
eous' – Matthew 5:45). A complete change of clothes makes
me presentable for a meeting of the parish hall committee.

♣ *Friday 8 April*

Today the world bids *adieu* to Pope John Paul II in a funeral
ranking with those of Winston Churchill and John F.
Kennedy. How marvellous (but not surprising) that while
millions were praying for the Holy Father during his last few
weeks this side of Heaven, he was praying for St Margaret's!

Last year a parishioner sent to the Vatican a copy of the
Ilkley Gazette containing a report and photograph following
my dedication in April of Graeme Willson's *The Madonna of
the Moors*. He felt the Pope would enjoy learning about the
painting in view of his high regard (which I share) for Mary
as *Theotokos* ('God-bearer') – a title bestowed by the early
Church to safeguard the doctrine of the divinity of Jesus.
Early in February a letter came back from a diplomat in the
Vatican's Secretariat of State, Monsignor Gabriele Caccia. It
reads:

> The Holy Father has received your letter and he has
> asked me to thank you. He appreciates the sentiments
> which prompted you to write to him.
>
> His Holiness will remember you and all associated
> with St Margaret's parish in his prayers and he invokes
> upon you God's blessings of joy and peace.

Holy Mary, *Theotokos* – pray for us sinners now and at the hour of *our* death.

❧ *Saturday 9 April*

It's 10 am on Grand National day, and a steady stream of once-a-year gamblers are crossing the threshold of Ilkley's betting shop.

There's at least a 7–1 chance against picking the winner, but over at the Winter Garden the odds in our Spring Fayre tombola are only 5–1. Most eyes are on the favourite, number 500 – the bottle of Teacher's Whisky.

The helpers start arriving around 8 am, and soon the place is a hive of activity. Cardboard boxes of books, clothes, plants and other items are carried in, and tables are set up on both levels. The elaborate railings on the first floor of this splendid building give it an air of a Harrogate tearoom; all that is lacking are the teacakes and musical trio.

As the time for the 'off' approaches, ladies circulate with cups of tea and coffee for the helpers. I find myself drawn to the white elephant stall, which reminds me of the 1895 Punch cartoon, 'The Curate's Egg':

> VICAR: I'm afraid you've got a bad egg there, Mr Jones.
> CURATE: Oh no, my Lord, I assure you! Parts of it are excellent!

Some good-humoured banter is directed at Lesley Ayres, a bubbly biology teacher with a slight Scouse accent, which takes me back to 1965–70, when I was Curate of St John's, Tuebrook, Liverpool. Lesley has brought for sale a decanter and glasses which slot into a model train playing *O Sole Mio* at the turn of a key. Some people admire her 'collectable', but

I would pay £100 to keep it out of the vicarage! Lesley has the last laugh, though, for by 10.01 am the train has gone for a fiver. As the old Latin saying goes, *De gustibus non est disputandum* ('there's no accounting for tastes')!

There's no doubt who are the busiest helpers – church stalwart Tony Klepper and his assistant Teresa Cannell on the tombola. Some regret that Teresa is not wearing the top hat which she occasionally dons on these occasions. My first few tickets produce only a can of lager, and there are smiles when I win luxury soap and body lotion, which I give to Teresa. Lesley is having a 'lorra, lorra luck' with her tickets – 'I can wash my hair, then put my feet up with wine and chocolates,' she beams. Suddenly, the Winter Garden erupts with laughter and cheers as, with my final try, I draw number 500 and walk off with the whisky!

I wonder – should I use my good fortune to illustrate a sermon on the text 'Hope does not disappoint ...' (Romans 5:5)? I'd better not prepare one on Nil Desperandum, though. Some parishioners may have lost their shirt on that horse, which finishes sixth in the National.

✤ Sunday 10 April

I take care not to announce any of the hymns as 'Number 500', but my mind is by now on another figure, 1,250 – the number of pounds brought in by the Spring Fayre, against £1,000 last year. It's a creditable amount, all the more so because there was competition in Ilkley yesterday from at least four similar events.

The General Election will soon be upon us, and today the parishioners have some practice in voting. There are 10 candidates, ranging from Mr B ('Up to £10,000' Party) to Mr K ('Over £80,000' Party). I'm reminded of Nikita Khrushchev, ex-leader of the former Soviet Union, who doubtless subscribed to the doctrine of the redistribution of wealth and whom, since he is dead, I cannot libel under our capitalist legal system.

Voters will be asked this week or next to declare how much annual income they have – rather than what they would like! The exercise is designed to help the Diocese to set the fairest possible shares for parishes next year. Each form has a 'tear across the dotted line' instruction, allowing name and signature to go in one box, and income in another. A note from Bishop David about the local share system praises the 'sterling' [sic] efforts which parishes make in trying to meet their targets.

I'm to be the Returning Officer, and am fairly confident there will be no ballot-rigging or any other malpractice. If you can't trust the Holy Spirit, operating through each Christian's conscience, who can you rely on?

♣ *Monday 11 April*

You are not likely to find a better example of a living faith than 'Gentleman' Alec Smith, aged 92 – well known locally for his bow ties – whom I am asked to anoint this evening at Troutbeck Nursing Home, half a mile from the vicarage. I say 'living' faith deliberately, because Alec is looking forward to death. Since moving into Troutbeck from his home a stone's throw from St Margaret's, he has grown increasingly frustrated at his deteriorating hearing and eyesight – and above all, perhaps, at his forgetting of words. 'He loved words,' says his son Christopher, formerly Canon Residentiary at Sheffield Cathedral and now Vicar of Doncaster Parish Church. 'But now he is ready to go home to God – he has no doubts about the reality of eternal life.'

I have only met Alec a couple of times, but in any case remind myself that the clergy can't afford to be over-emotional on such occasions so I get on with the task in hand. Making the sign of the Cross in oil on Alec's forehead, I say:

> 'Alec, I anoint you with oil in the name of our Lord
>   Jesus Christ.
> May the Lord in his love and mercy uphold you
> by the grace and power of the Holy Spirit.'

I suspect Alec is hardly, if at all, aware of what is going on – especially in view of his profound deafness. But I continue:

> 'As you are outwardly anointed with this holy oil,
> so may our heavenly Father grant you
> the inward anointing of the Holy Spirit.
> Of his great mercy
> may he forgive you your sins
> and release you from suffering.
> May he deliver you from all evil,
> preserve you in all goodness
> and bring you to everlasting life;
> through Jesus Christ our Lord.'

The final prayer, from the Western Rite of Commendation, will be familiar to those who know Elgar's *Dream of Gerontius*:

> 'Alec, go forth upon your journey from this world,
> in the name of God the Father almighty who created you;
> in the name of Jesus Christ who suffered death for you;
> in the name of the Holy Spirit who strengthens you;
> in communion with the blessed saints,
> and aided by angels and archangels,
> and all the armies of the heavenly host.
> May your portion this day be in peace,
> and your dwelling the heavenly Jerusalem.'

✿ *Tuesday 12 April*

My first meeting with the Parochial Church Council (PCC). I don't like endless, circular chatter so Anne Kilvington, the secretary, has sent round a notice saying the meeting will start at 7.45 pm, should conclude by 9 pm and will certainly be over by 9.30 pm. At the meeting I tell everyone I like crisp comments, and if anyone wants to carry on talking after 9.30 pm that's fine but I won't be there. With Anne on my side, I am not expecting much opposition to this. Anne is kind, but used to dealing with potential trouble-makers, having been a history teacher and head of the sixth form at Skipton Girls High School. You might describe her as a wolf in cuddly sheep's clothing – we asked her permission to do so.

There's a good spirit among the PCC members, but it proves difficult to meet at the back of the church rather than in a hall: in view of the way the chairs were set out, there's no real eye contact. This is no one's fault, and we'll get it right next time. I am sure the PCC will be more effective if we have only a small number of discussion papers each time and they are sent out in advance. As it is, tonight there's too much speaking 'cold' to too many reports and we don't get round to the re-marriage of divorcees until 9.25 pm. The subject is not to be entered into lightly, so is postponed. Before we break up, I say that if St Margaret's is to proclaim and live the Gospel of hope for all through the love of God in Christ, the PCC should become more of a mission team which leaves the 'nuts and bolts' to others. The early Church adopted this approach in appointing deacons to support the apostles (Acts 6:1).

✿ *Wednesday 13 April*

To the Town Hall, to meet the Chairman of Ilkley Parish Council, Councillor Brian Mann. He shows me the Council

Chamber, which is impressive.

I raise the possibility of double yellow lines being introduced in the area around St Margaret's, which is often congested. Councillor Mann suggests I write to Bradford Council and allow the 'due process' to run. On reflection, we can't really argue that we're a special case – everywhere you look in Ilkley there seem to be traffic problems. Much anxiety surrounds the A65 Skipton–Leeds road at its junction (where there are traffic lights) with Victoria Avenue on the western edge of the town. Many local residents are complaining about delays caused by cars turning right into Victoria Avenue, while others feel the yellow lines in Victoria Avenue should be extended to reduce the risk of accidents caused by vehicles colliding in a confined space.

This week's regular ecumenical clerical lunch is *chez Hope*. All Saints Vicar Paul Tudge has told me to expect six visitors, but there are about nine – most have already met me, so I suppose the extra bods are here to case the fairly new vicarage joint. We dine *el cheapo* – not *al fresco,* but *el Tesco* – on large tins of soup, bread, cheese, biscuits and fruit.

❧ *Thursday 14 April*

> 65 today, 65 today;
> he has the key of the vicarage door,
> never had a wheelie-bin before …

To Rombalds Hotel, just opposite the vicarage, for lunch with my twin sister Anne, her husband Peter and my niece Suzanne. They come back afterwards for a while, and then I get on with preparations for Sunday.

❧ *Saturday 16 April*

There's a surprise for the Ilkley group of the University of the Third Age ('U3A'), an organisation offering education for older people. They have heard I am to talk on 'The Sea', and some members have wondered whether this will be Dead, Red or Med! In fact, my topic is 'The See', primarily giving a picture of my time as Archbishop but also touching on my work as Bishop of Wakefield and Bishop of London.

Of course, both life at sea and in the See can be turbulent at times – especially since sections of the press tend to emphasise (thereby increasing) the tensions between 'evangelical' and 'catholic' Anglicans. Such stereotyping is an oversimplification and rather an insult to God for, as St Paul says, 'each of us was given grace according to the measure of Christ's gift' (Ephesians 4:7). If, as the apostle says, there is 'one Lord, one faith, one baptism' (Ephesians 4:5), then all Christians should acknowledge both the catholicity (universal nature) of the Church and the priority of evangelising. Reverting to the Sea/See theme, perhaps the only differentiation Christians should admit to is one between 'drys' and 'wets' – those with a sense of humour and those without!

❧ *Sunday 17 April*

One of the pleasures (or compensations) of becoming an OAP is that you're entitled to a bus pass. Mine is a very special one. It comes this morning, made of marzipan, on a cake that appears mysteriously at the back of the church after the 10.30 am Eucharist.

I am saying goodbye to those not staying for coffee when suddenly Fr Alan Brown launches into 'Happy Birthday' in his rich, fruitcake-mixture voice and everyone joins in. There aren't any candles on the cake – perhaps because they celebrated Candlemas in February. It's a light, delicious sponge cake, and they kindly give me the remaining half to take home. I know Marie Anson is on the Social Committee, but wasn't aware her middle name was Antoinette! In fact, to be fair to Queen Marie Antoinette, she never said: 'Let them eat cake!' The eminent historian Antonia Fraser attributes a remark on these lines to Maria Theresa, the Spanish wife of Louis XIV.

By a happy coincidence Thursday was also the birthday of Teresa Cannell, who gets the 'Happy Birthday' treatment too. In view of all the cakes I've been given in Ilkley, you might think I've put on weight. In fact, I have lost a bit. The town is quite hilly, and I've done a lot of walking – mainly on the five-minute down-up between the vicarage and the church.

The share-weighting exercise has gone well. There are 156 response forms in, while 22 people were assessed without a form, making 178. Since the Electoral Roll contains 190 names, the turnout is almost 94 per cent! There are no spoiled ballot papers and no reports of gerrymandering (e.g. by other churches offering to give us their collection). Anne Kilvington took the 'tops' and I totted up the 'bottoms'. The numbers match exactly – what a bright lot I've got!

❧ Monday 18 April

On the train to London, where tomorrow I'm to be involved in the Memorial Service for Lord Hanson, who as James Hanson built the Hanson Trust into one of Britain's most powerful companies. I knew him quite well, and we received an honorary degree at the same time. According to *The Times*, he had 'a passion for parties and beautiful women', having dated Jean Simmons, Joan Collins and Audrey Hepburn. In 1988, Wakefield Diocese's centenary year, he kindly let me borrow a helicopter for a day and I hurried from school to school, descending like God from on high.

The Hanson family take me out for a private lunch and put me up at the 5-star Berkeley Hotel. It has a huge amount to offer – indoor/outdoor pool, CD and film library, steam room, shoe-shine service and video-conference facilities, to name but a few. Sadly, I'm too late in life for the beauty salon, and had better not avail myself of the twice-daily maid service (you know what the press are like). My room, which overlooks Hyde Park, is opulent, with a balcony and terrace, air-conditioning, kitchenette, and fridge with mini-bar. Something is missing, however – tea-making facilities. I have to ring up to get someone to fetch me a cuppa.

✤ *Tuesday 19 April*

St Paul's, Knightsbridge, is packed with celebrities for the Memorial Service. The Revd Alan Gyle, the Vicar, officiates, while I lead the prayers and give the Blessing. Among the household names are (in alphabetical order) Jonathan Aitken, Lord Archer, Alan Bennett, Sir Michael Caine, Lord Patten and Richard Whiteley. Most eyes, however, are on Lady Thatcher, whom I speak with briefly afterwards. She looks frail but is still very sharp. Memorials are important – the Holy Eucharist itself is an act of commemoration – but life stands still for no one, and part of my mind today is with another family in mourning: that of Alec Smith, who died yesterday. I'm to take his funeral next week.

I wonder why the press are so obsessed with dogs these days? First, they give acres of space to those dubbing Tony Blair the 'poodle' of George 'Dubya' Bush. Currently, in view of the newly elected Pope's reputation as a conservative, they are reporting claims that he has been a 'Rottweiler'. To my mind, mud-slinging usually damages the throwers rather than the target. Cardinal Ratzinger is a brilliant theologian; in choosing him, the Cardinals may have opted for a period of stability while they consider new options.

What all the Christian churches need, of course, is a different breed of dog – one bringing mercy, relief and refreshment to those in need. In short, a St Bernard. As I prepare for a short post-Easter break in the Dales, I reflect on how lucky we are in having such a loyal, loving toiler for the Lord as Canon Bernard Gribbin, who was a priest for 36 years (21 in the Bradford Diocese) before he retired nine years ago.

Since moving to Ilkley 18 months ago, Fr Bernard has energised the Family Service by introducing more singable hymns with 'action' choruses. Among other things, he has helped with the choir, run a successful stewardship campaign, and created our Christmas cards. Bernard has belonged to the College of Preachers for 35 years, and can give 'short but sweet' sermons – at Chester Cathedral, the maximum length allowed during the Sung Eucharist was six sentences!

The pressures on parish priests can easily take their toll, so it's good to have such a cheerful and experienced priest helping out so doggedly.

❧ *Sunday 24 April*

> 'Take, eat; this is my body.' (Mark 14:22)

> 'Take this, Ellie – it's Bonio!'

What a difference Holy Communion can make. Those who seem tired or worried going up to the altar rail often smile on the way back to their seats – sometimes with a positive spring in their step. A bound is more appropriate in the case of Ellie, a nine-year-old golden retriever. She knows that her owner, Angela Halton, will soon be retrieving a dog-biscuit from her coat pocket when they're back in their usual place next to the aisle, where Ellie can most easily take in what's going on, and perhaps doze lightly during the sermon (don't even think about it!).

Angela, now 62, has been virtually blind through diabetes since 1993, two years before her husband Tim, a graphic arts manager, died from Alzheimer's Disease on Christmas Day. As time passes, the day becomes easier for her to get through – having her two grandchildren around helps. But she says the pain of losing her husband on this most special day will never go completely, even though, she says, 'I'm not bitter – there are people with greater burdens to bear.'

Angela has another sad memory – her younger son, Christopher, was killed in a road accident in 1985, aged only 18. He had passed his test that day on a 150 cc motorbike, and borrowed a 1000 cc machine to come home on:

> He ran into a car coming the other way on a bad bend on the moor road. He was on the wrong side of the road – maybe the bike was too big for him to handle. With Tim, I was expecting it because he had been ill for 10 years, but Christopher ... he went out of the door one evening, and didn't come back.

Despite the trauma of losing Christopher, Angela put into practice her belief in 'getting on with things'. Next day, as an Ilkley Brown Owl, she took 24 Brownies by bus to join 60,000 others attending a celebration at Harrogate Showground to mark 75 years of Guiding.

Angela's Christian faith has not been shaken by the triple blow of losing her sight, husband and son. She says that, if anything, it has forced her to reflect more on the mystery that, in Jesus, God came among humanity's suffering to share it – and still suffers when men, women and children are afflicted. God was 'very close' to her when Christopher died, shortly after Tim had been diagnosed with Alzheimer's:

He was just there all the time – I felt cushioned, as though I was in the clouds and God was all around me. It was not the same when Tim died – maybe because the pain was less intense for a longer period and I was not in such immediate need.

Angela has many good friends, like Clare Heap, who drives her and Ellie up to Ilkley Moor for walks (Angela's blindness came on gradually; giving up driving was particularly hard). Clare also takes them to St Margaret's on Sundays. By a huge stroke of irony, Ellie was born on 3 January 1996, the day Tim was cremated.

Angela says:

> If I say to Ellie, 'I'm going to change for a walk', she will sit at the bottom of the stairs and wait, knowing we're going out. When Clare arrives, she goes mad. Clare hangs on to me on the moor, and the dog rushes about for an hour – I suppose she has to let off steam somehow. After all this time, she knows me very well – there's a kind of telepathy between us. I believe that when I die, I shall meet all my family, lots of friends – and Ellie.

❧ *Monday 25 April*

It's funny how a change of scene can sometimes throw a whole new light on someone's character.

When she is preaching or leading the prayers in church, Lay Reader Catherine Gibson is transparently devout, and anyone meeting her for the first time might label her as meek and mild. But Miss Hyde turns into Dr Jekyll at St Margaret's Burns Supper in January when, I am told, Catherine uses a dirk to commit GBH with considerable gusto on a poor defenceless haggis. I am looking forward to next year's event which, God willing, will be in our new parish hall! I had to decline an invitation last year as it coincided with my winding-down as Archbishop.

For 12 nights this month, Catherine has a leading role in the production by the Ilkley Players at Ilkley Playhouse of Terence Frisby's *Rough Justice*, in which a 'Jeremy Paxman'-type TV personality is on trial for the murder of his 'cabbage' of a child. One performance was attended by a group of 78 magistrates, many of whom apparently disagreed with the jury's verdict!

Catherine puts in such a powerful performance in her long and demanding role as Margaret Casely, QC, the Prosecutor, that for once 'Paxo' is well and truly trussed up, stuffed and roasted! A group from St Margaret's who attended the production wonder how Catherine managed to learn so many lines! Her secret is 'karaoke' – she recorded the other actors' words and spoke her own part against them.

Catherine, a former college librarian who retired early, leads a busy life in and out of church (for a start, she belongs to two choirs) but is in church every day for both Morning and Evening Prayer in addition to the Sunday services. Sometimes she and I are the only two at worship, so I must take care if at some point this imaginative lady lands a role in *Murder in the Cathedral* – I'm told she takes rehearsals very seriously.

♣ *Tuesday 26 April*

Alec Smith witnessed to his Christian faith in life – including to me during his last weeks – and now he is witnessing through his family's death notice in the *Ilkley Gazette*, which concludes:

Alleluia, Christ is risen! He is risen indeed, Alleluia!

Tonight Alec's body is being received into church prior to the Funeral and Requiem tomorrow. Canon Christopher Smith says the Reception is helpful in making the process of saying to his father 'goodbye for now' more meaningful and reflective.

Six large candles surround the two trestles on which the coffin is to be placed. The air is heavy with the scent of lilies as, carrying the cross, I follow the choir, who lead the procession into church singing the Burial Sentences impeccably and unaccompanied.

Christopher says: 'For love of Alec and for each of us, Lord, you bore our sins on the Cross.' On the west wall of the church, on one of the Stations of the Cross, Jesus lies powerless on the ground while two Roman soldiers hold him down and a third smashes nails into his wrists with a hammer. I read a lesson about this 'amazing grace' taken from Romans 8:31–39:

> I am convinced that neither death, nor life … nor anything else in all creation, will be able to separate us from the love of God in Christ Jesus our Lord.

After several psalms and prayers, I close the short service with the grace. Some mourners light candles and remain behind for private prayers, but the church is to be locked overnight.

🍀 Wednesday 27 April

Where do I begin – to tell the story of how great a love can be?

That was an easy question for Fr Alan Brown as he wrote the address for Alec Smith's Funeral Requiem today – it all began with an orange. Alan says Alec was a smart, stylish dresser and dancer whose hero was Fred Astaire. When his wife-to-be, Marjorie, met him in the insurance office where they both worked, he seemed 'a bit of a lounge lizard'. On being teased, she threw an orange at him – but his interest was to bear fruit. Alec served on the wartime Atlantic and Russian convoys, almost being torpedoed several times. As an officer based in Portsmouth, he helped preparations for the invasion of France, with Marjorie nearby as a telephonist. After a highly successful marriage, Alec found her death in 1997 hard to bear, but kept up his daily routine of praying for others.

Fr Alan concludes:

> We have no way of measuring time or age in the eternal sphere. If we could gaze directly into the heavenly realm, what would we see – a younger Alec dancing like Fred Astaire, with Marjorie as his Ginger Rogers? Or a slightly more mature couple, intertwined in that love which comes from knowing and caring for each other for over 50 years? Who knows? But in faith, I am sure he is in that nearer presence of God – Father, Son and Holy Spirit – and in that nearer presence will be worshipping his beloved Lord.

❧ Thursday 28 April

Jesus is coming for me shortly; I had this on good authority last night from Steve Boggan, of *The Times*, who arrived for an interview today. Naturally I was somewhat surprised and said: 'What do you mean?' Steve explained that this Jesus was Victor Manuel Christo de Jesus, a freelance photographer, who would be joining us at our appointment.

'Foxes have holes, and birds of the air have nests; but the Son of Man has nowhere to lay his head' (Luke 9:58). Steve, by contrast, laid his head last night at the Craiglands, Ilkley's most exclusive hotel, overlooking the moor. It's a popular spot for weddings, although it can expect to lose some trade when our new parish hall is built, can't it?

Steve and Victor stay with me most of the morning. Victor is rather happy-snappy, and takes around 100 photos – mostly on the moor and inside the vicarage. His face is familiar, and he reminds me that we met when a portrait of me was unveiled at Bishopthorpe. He was born in London of Portuguese parents, and is 30 – roughly the same age as Jesus was when he began his ministry (Luke 3:23).

✂ *Friday 29 April*

The second coming of Jesus. Sorry about that, but there are hints in the Gospels that *the* Jesus had a sense of humour, for example his references to 'the plank in your eye' (Matthew 7:5) and 'a camel going through the eye of a needle' (Mark 10:25). Victor de Jesus says he was teased about his name at primary school, but these days most people meeting him for the first time merely remark: 'I expect you've heard every joke going ...'

Lacking omniscience, Victor didn't realise that those in authority (i.e. *The Times* picture desk) wanted some shots of me outside the vicarage and others in front of St Margaret's. They might have given Jesus precise instructions. What did they expect – a miracle? Anyway, Victor rings me up early today and we spend another 20 minutes or so pacifying the picture editor.

After lunch I have a meeting with Jane Hickson (producer) and Ian Clayton (presenter) from Yorkshire Television, who want me to appear in a programme in their series *My Yorkshire*. I met Ian as Archbishop when I supported an appeal by St George's Crypt, a refuge in Leeds for the homeless.

Filming is to be divided between Wakefield, where I grew up, and Flamborough Head – that beautiful home of puffins on the East Coast.

🎬 Saturday 30 April

Our church has a large number of talented musicians, who tonight put on a concert for Christian Aid.

It's organised by Ruth Cheney and her sister Nadine Wharton, both former students of the Royal College of Music. Ruth was Principal Viola with the Innsbruck Symphony Orchestra, then Sub-Principal of the Rotterdam Philharmonic, while her cellist sister has played with the BBC Scottish Symphony Orchestra, BBC Philharmonic, Liverpool Philharmonic and Northern Sinfonia. They are part of a remarkable musical family who make up two string quartets and hope some day to play the Mendelssohn Octet.

Tonight's performers include Jude Cooke (17) and his 12-year-old brother Tristram, two gifted singers. Jude has been in St Margaret's Choir for seven years – until his voice broke, as sole treble in a sea (it's that word again) of sopranos. He has just been accepted as a tenor in the National Youth Choir. Tristram has been a chorister at Ripon Cathedral for three years. Before becoming a boarder at the Choir School, he played the violin and served at our Family Service. In the holidays he sings in our choir – again as the only treble. It's a busman's holiday for someone who sings in services every day, but Tristram is a bundle of energy. Among his interests is everything French – especially Napoleon! Today he is given special permission to leave Evensong at Ripon after the anthem.

Stuart Hanson, son of our social committee chairman, Anne Hanson, and her husband, Malcolm, gives another fine tenor performance, while head server John Sunderland rounds the evening off with his accordion. It has been a most enjoyable evening, and raises £275.

May

🎋 Sunday 1 May

As in many churches, we shake hands in friendship during the Peace at our main Sunday Eucharist.

Today, though, one member of the congregation seems to be shaking more hands than is normal – it's as though he's addicted to the practice. Yes, this is barrister James Keeley, Liberal Democrat candidate for Pudsey, for whom there are now only four more hand-pumping days until the General Election, which this year coincides with Ascension Day.

James estimates he has shaken hundreds of hands during the campaign, but draws the line at kissing babies. 'It's not something I feel comfortable about', he confesses. Not surprisingly James is not in church at 3 pm, when I baptise Caitlin Eloise, daughter of PCC member Dr Carmel Ramage and her husband Christopher. Instead, he's listening to the Settle Orchestra. His wife Tracy is leader of the amateur orchestra, whose programme today includes Sibelius' Symphony No. 2.

Three weeks ago James was jumped on outside Pudsey Market by two women – one elderly, the other in her twenties – who inflicted upon him actual bodily kissing. 'I'm not sure if it's my personal charm, but it's one of the hazards a would-be MP must face – ladies can vote; babies can't,' he says.

❧ *Tuesday 3 May*

There's more than average interest in politics here as the General Election approaches. Ilkley is a small town of around 14,000 residents in the Keighley constituency. There's a great contrast between Ilkley and the town of Keighley, whose population is about 70,000. Ilkley is largely a base for professional people commuting to Leeds or Bradford; most people live comfortably, and according to a recent survey the town has more millionaires for its size than anywhere else in Yorkshire. There are few non-white residents. Keighley, by contrast, has a sizeable Asian population and above-average unemployment.

After a fair showing by his party in the local elections last year, British National Party leader Nick Griffin is to stand in this constituency on Thursday. An anti-BNP campaign involving churches, mosques, trade unionists and others advocating racial harmony has been organised under the umbrella of the Keighley Together organisation. In Ilkley, Churches Together in Ilkley has issued a leaflet calling for racial harmony without mentioning the BNP by name.

❧ *Wednesday 4 May*

A regular feature of St Margaret's twice-yearly church fayres could soon be on the way out, having become, like itself, a white elephant.

For several years parishioners have taken all sorts of items to that stall: crockery, pens, suitcases … everything but the kitchen sink (no doubt someone will claim to have sold one in 1980). Some of these have found buyers, but a great many have been taken to charity shops or the Council tip in Golden Butts Road.

Tonight the social committee decides not to have a white

elephant stall at this year's Christmas Fayre but to ask church members to bring back something from their holidays for a holiday souvenir stall. The committee hope people will exercise good taste and not bring back tack from Clacton-on-Sea or something naff from Nafferton, Driffield.

I suppose the test when buying is: would you select one for your mother/father/daughter/son – or mother-in-law?

Thursday 5 May
ASCENSION DAY

Back to where I once belonged – no, not Liverpool but Bishopthorpe Palace for a buffet lunch for Anne Broadbent, my former secretary, who is retiring. It seems strange to be there again. I say a few words and chat to people for a while, but am thankful not to be returning full-time – Bishopthorpe is an impossible place to live in. The Archbishop's rooms are spread about one side of the house which, whenever there's a formal function, tends to be invaded by catering and other staff. I was acutely aware of the lack of personal space for the Archbishop – vital in view of the demands which come with the position – and do hope this problem will be addressed so that my successor can receive better privacy.

Ascension is such an under-rated festival, in view of its astonishing message that the exultation of Christ's humanity to the heights of Heaven is an assurance of our being raised to glory, glimpses of which are given at every Eucharist. As Bishop Christopher Wordsworth puts it in his hymn 'See, the Conqueror Mounts in Triumph':

> Jesus reigns, adored by angels;
> man with God is on the throne;
> Mighty Lord, in Thine ascension
> we by faith behold our own.

or as St Irenaeus, the early Church Father, expressed it:

> He became like we are that we might become as he is.

I believe that God *is* 'working his purpose out', as a hymn declares, and that in the end his Kingdom will come. Despite much evil in the world, there have been positive signs in recent years – like the Jubilee 2000 campaign and now Make Poverty History, in which the Holy Spirit has been working through religious people and others of good will. I'm not wild about the General Election, though. The world won't change overnight, whatever the result, and I'm bored with politicians and their shenanigans. And so to bed – at 10.30 pm!

☙ *Friday 6 May*

The heat has been on Ann Cryer, the Labour candidate for Keighley, who has been defending a majority of 4,005. It has come from the BNP, which has conducted an aggressive campaign aimed mainly at Ann, a Christian Socialist, who worships occasionally with us.

But unknown to all her opponents, the Labour candidate has two special heavyweights on her side. They are her late husbands – Bob Cryer, killed in a road accident in 1994, and Anglican clergyman the Revd John Hammersley, who died from cancer only in November. Ann says that at difficult times in her life either Bob or John has been there for her. She is sure this is not wishful thinking on her part or a memory of what they might have advised if they were with her physically – it is something from the Beyond.

Ann says:

> Sometimes I've been standing up facing a difficult question and my reaction has been, 'What would Bob

be saying?' Then my voice has started to answer, and I've felt Bob was there influencing me. It happens more with John now. He says: 'It's not complicated. Tell them what you think – you're good at that!' John is with me a great deal of the time.

Since 1999 Ann has been surrounded by controversy for her stance on racial issues. She has spoken out against forced marriages, condemned the beating of children in a minority of Islamic evening schools and said Asians should be encouraged to learn English as a second language: she estimates that half of the Asians in and around Bradford cannot speak it.

As a result, she has been condemned by a minority of Asian leaders, while some Asian Labour councillors even called for her to be expelled from the party. Whatever your politics, you have to admire her courage in speaking out on the sensitive issue of race.

Ann says:

> I have been called a racist and an Islamophobe, and this is particularly hurtful to someone with three half-Indian grandchildren. All I have done is to call for positive solutions to real problems. I think the BNP decided to stand against me because I was a threat to their negative ideas – they were happy simply to raise matters and let things fester.

In the early hours Ann retains her seat with a majority of 4,852. The BNP receives 9.2 per cent of the vote, with Labour down 3.5 per cent, the Tories down 4.7 per cent and the Lib Dems up 0.9 per cent. 'I think the presence of Nick Griffin encouraged traditional Labour voters who might otherwise have stayed at home to turn out,' she suggests.

Over at Leeds Civic Hall, James Keeley makes a fighting

speech after picking up 4.2 per cent more votes for the Lib Dems but still coming third. 'Our beliefs are strong and true. We will fight in every nook and cranny of this constituency to win next time,' he declares. One local newspaper says he is clearly disappointed by his share of the vote, while another declares he's delighted. After four weeks of non-stop campaigning, James is just thankful to be back in bed at 5 am after some final Election kisses – from his wife and his 19-month-old daughter, Alexandra.

♣ Sunday 8 May

It's exactly 60 years since VE Day, and at the suggestion of Ilkley Parish Council the Revd Brian Gregory, Vicar of St John's, Ben Rhydding, has arranged a local celebration to coincide with many taking place nationally. The Memorial Gardens is the intended venue, but it's raining so we head for the Baptist Church Hall nearby. The hall is like an air-raid shelter – Baptist minister Stuart Jenkins says it is 'pristine in its 1940s condition'.

I had the impression there'd be a short service followed by entertainment, but instead there's an intermingling of prayers, period songs, reminiscences and more prayers. The Leader of the Revels, Shirley Britton, is impressive. She goes round the circle of chairs, singing old 'sweetheart' songs at the old blokes and inviting them to sing and dance with her. She asks: 'Do you remember [so-and-so] or [such-and-such] ...?' Having been born just a few weeks before Dunkirk, I have virtually no memory of the war – not even of rationing. But I do recall the gas masks (mine included), the sirens and our bomb shelter downstairs in the cellar. It was built by my father from a couple of rolled steel joists ('RSJs'), and I know we went into it at least once.

For me, today's celebration ends up more like Dunkirk

than VE Day. I've an appointment at 4.15 pm, but Shirley is still going strong at 4.05 pm – giving the impression she can carry on until bedtime. She moves towards me with a glint in her eye, so I make what was called early on in the war a 'strategic withdrawal' – as investigators on mass-circulation Sunday newspapers used to say in the 1950s: 'I made my excuses and left.'

The *Ilkley Gazette* later reported:

> [Shirley] sang 'Slow Boat to China' and 'A Nightingale Sang in Berkeley Square' at the same time wooing, to their embarrassment, but to the obvious delight of her audience, some of the eminent guests present, among them Father David Hope, of St Margaret's Church, and Councillor Mike Gibbons.

❧ *Monday 9 May*

During the afternoon of 20 July 2003 – St Margaret's Patronal Festival – fire broke out in a wastepaper bin in the choir vestry, which is reached via steps at the back of the church. By good fortune the solid door was closed so only smoke penetrated the church itself, but even so the total damage amounted to £60,000. The cause was never discovered.

Unfortunately, visitors from several parishes in the Wakefield Diocese had chosen that day to attend Evensong here. Those who were ex-miners with breathing problems stood in the porch away from the smoke. The organ was out of action and the service took place by candlelight – with difficulty, since nearly all the choir's hymn books and sheets had been destroyed. Fr Bernard climbed the pulpit gingerly for the sermon and likened himself to Wee Willie Winkie!

This year the PCC decided to arrange training in fire prevention for a small team. A course was organised by Brian

Whittam, appointed as Health and Safety Officer, but the first meeting was a damp squib. Minutes before the start, the trainer rang to say he'd lost the keys to his van and his wife had left for work with the spares in her handbag. Today the course goes ahead successfully, with full training in the theory and practice of fire prevention.

Everyone passed the exam, but the Verger, Adrian Robinson, said it was the first he'd sat where no one had cheated!

✤ Tuesday 10 May

Tonight the PCC is discussing the issue of the re-marriage of divorcees in church.

The Church of England teaches that marriage is for life but that some marriages do, sadly, fail and in these cases it seeks to be 'available' for all involved. Only in 'exceptional circumstances' may a divorced person re-marry in church during the lifetime of a former spouse.

At our meeting some strong views are expressed both ways, but the PCC recognises that in the end the decision will be mine: the law permits a priest not to take such a marriage on grounds of conscience. Personally, I would prefer those wishing to re-marry in church to be committed Christians and that normally we should continue with the blessing of marriages following a civil ceremony.

✤ Wednesday 11 May

After lunch I'm in Skipton to meet John Dawson, General Secretary of the Skipton Building Society, who has written inviting me to join the trustees of their charity, which needs people from outside the financial world. I accept the invitation. The next meeting is in the autumn; I wonder if there's time to re-name our new parish hall appeal the Ilkley Vicarious Liability Benevolent Society?

Joking apart, things are only getting better. I've recently received £1,000 from *The Mail on Sunday* for 1,000 words they published following an interview I gave to a staff member. Of course, the cheque was made payable to St Margaret's PCC!

☙ *Friday 13 May*

Today I conduct my first funeral service at Skipton Crematorium. I seem to spend most of the time pressing buttons – one to close the curtains; another to get someone to put on a record. There's a delay between pressing the button and hearing the music, and I can't help wondering if something has gone wrong. Has he gone to sleep? Has he gone for a walk? Has he just forgotten to put it on? It's a great relief when Rutter's *Celtic Blessing* comes on. Skipton Crem is reasonable as they go, but in general I find these places depressing – they try to be 'all things to all people' and in the process often become nothing to anybody.

Today parishioner Mave Cockcroft is 80. I pop round to her flat after lunch, but she's out – as usual. Mave is one of our most sociable parishioners, with a huge circle of friends at home and abroad, and is a brick to those who are ill. During the war she was a Leading Wren in the Portsmouth Division and worked on the camouflaging of tanks in the Havant forest before the D-Day landings. She sounds posh but is quite normal and good fun. A friend who went with her to see Mel Gibson's *The Passion of the Christ* in Leeds teased her by insisting they meet outside the Upper Crust café at Leeds Station. They were so moved by the realistic ultra-violence of the film that they unwound afterwards with an Irish whiskey each!

❧ *Sunday 15 May*
PENTECOST

> 'Here is the Lamb of God who takes away the sin of the
> world!' (John 1:29)

Eighteen-month-old Louis Allen is not just beholding the
lamb on our huge painting *The Madonna of the Moors* above
the font. It seems he'd like to snatch it from John the Baptist's
hands and take it home as a pet.

Today is Pentecost – the birthday of the Church, when
God's Holy Spirit came down suddenly upon the first
Christians, giving them courage to proclaim to a largely hos-
tile world the unexpected Good News of the crucified and
risen Jesus as the answer to humanity's fears and sins. He still
is!

It's an extra-special day, because the toddler being baptised
is very special. Louis was born in December 2003 to Deborah
and Philip, a solicitor working in Leeds. He had a hole-in-
the-heart condition and an exomphalos ('*ex*', 'out of";
'*omphalos*', 'navel' [Greek]), a condition which caused several
internal organs to be outside his body in a sac the size of a
baseball. Louis spent over four months in the neo-natal and
cardiac units at Leeds General Infirmary while surgeons
operated on him.

Phil says:

> Although hole-in-the-heart operations are regarded as
> fairly routine these days, an exomphalos is more com-
> plicated to deal with. However, Deb and I were fairly
> calm – we felt we could trust the medical staff.

The couple are naturally full of joy when today, thanks to the
wonders of modern technology, Louis is a strong and healthy-

looking boy weighing about 20lbs. He knows he's the centre of attention – and is loving it – while our very own Val and Tony Banks are pleased as Punch to be among the godparents!

After Phil, Deb and the godparents have promised to reject evil and follow Christ on behalf of Louis, they turn round and walk in procession to the font at the back. Louis is such a weight that Phil holds him during the moment of christening – he could easily have jumped out of my arms. His dad finds it easiest to suspend him backwards and upside down while I daub him with holy water. I thought this would set him off yelling, but it doesn't. It's good of Phil to take Louis to meet the congregation during the Peace in the Eucharist which follows the Baptism. Normal service is soon resumed back home in Burley-in-Wharfedale. Phil says:

> Louis looks at you when he's doing something wrong, listens when you are telling him off, does it again – and laughs at you. He runs around like any normal toddler. We are so pleased he is well now.

I hope the parents, and in particular the godparents, will remember their promises to pray for Louis. Today was a high for everyone, but when all concerned have come down from the mountain, it will not always be as easy. Christianity is not, and never can be, for 'in here', as it were – for those occasions when we are feeling particularly churchy or religious. It's just as much for those times when we are feeling up against it; when we are disheartened and fed up; for those times when we might be tempted to do a shady deal or two, to tell the odd lie because really it doesn't matter – when actually it does matter. It's a faith too which encourages us to take seriously the values of family life; to ensure the well-being of our neighbour as well as ourselves, sometimes at a considerable cost to ourselves.

❧ *Monday 16 May*

It's Day 2 of Christian Aid Week, and up and down the country a minority are polishing their excuses for giving little or nothing to help the poor.

Nadine Wharton, our CA Co-ordinator, has been collecting the comments as well as the cash. Here's a selection:

- Have you got some change?
- Sorry – I have done my charity for today.
- I don't do the religious bit but I'll take the leaflet on trade justice.
- You deserve something for walking up all those stairs.
- Do you really want me to give it to you now?
- I don't think I will, but thank you for giving me the opportunity.

Of course, it would be unkind and unfair to sit in judgement on anyone, as we don't know people's personal circumstances. Most people in Ilkley who are approached make at least a modest donation and there are many examples of great generosity. Nadine is particularly moved when a donor who has had a throat operation rushes inside for a microphone, which she places next to her neck. 'Sorry I can't speak properly – so nice of you to call,' she says cheerfully.

❧ *Wednesday 18 May*

Work on the new parish hall is just a week behind schedule due to extra pile-driving, and is now expected to be completed at the end of August. Now the attention of the project team switches to the nitty-gritty of chairs, floor-coverings, cupboards and so on. When we started we expected to have a shortfall on completion of £135,000, but thanks to extra grants, donations and fund-raising, the latest prediction is £111,000, which we shall need to borrow.

Our canny parish hall project director, Bryan Anson, and his team don't miss a trick: parishioners are to be asked to consider giving the cost of a particular item. For example, a dishwasher costs £1,890 (£1,475 under Gift Aid), curtains £1,600 (£1,250) while it is £40 (£31) for two holly trees. I dare say the project team would sound out Holly and Ivy if we had any members with those names!

❧ Thursday 19 May

This evening, at St Peter's Shipley, there's the Archdeacon's Visitation – a service for the swearing-in of churchwardens. Barbara France has held the office for several years, and probably knows the service by heart. John Baggaley, who is new to the position, is away in Norway so will have to go to the next occasion.

David Lee's sermon has three points and lasts for 10–12 minutes. Just right, in my opinion – if you waffle on too long, people drift into dreamland!

❧ Friday 20 May

One of the Church's most powerful hymns is sung in January at Epiphany, which celebrates the 'showing-forth' of Christ to the non-Jewish world, represented by the Magi (Matthew 2:1–12). It reminds us of the remarkable risks God took by sharing our humanity in Jesus. As J. M. Neale's 'Over the Hill and Over the Dale' puts it:

> He is God ye go to meet,
> therefore incense proffer.
> He is king ye go to greet;

gold is in your coffer.
Also, man, he comes to share
every woe that men can bear:
tempter, railer, scoffer.
Therefore now against the day
in the grave when him they lay,
myrrh ye also offer ...

This afternoon I'm at the BUPA hospital in Roundhay, Leeds, to visit Pam Hearnshaw – someone who really needs this sharing, and for whom Christ's 'comfortable words' might have been specially spoken:

'Come to me, all you that are weary and are carrying heavy burdens, and I will give you rest.'

(Matthew 11:28)

For several years now, Pam has lived daily with the grief of watching her husband Trevor, a former academic, descend deeper into Alzheimer's, which has left him unable to talk and in need of 24-hour care. He's a shell of his former self.

With considerable support from family, friends and carers, Pam has found the courage to bear her sad burden bravely, and often with humour. Two years ago on Mothering Sunday, Hugh's daughter Sarah (then 16) looked at Pam and Trevor in church, and said:

'You can forget Valentines and Mother's Day – real love is over there!'

Partly due to the physical demands made upon her by Trevor's condition, Pam has endured terrible pains in her legs. She's just had a hip replacement and is due for operations on both knees in September.

Not surprisingly, Trevor is being cared for in a home while

Pam is in hospital. Would you credit it? Pam is having to pay for him to be looked after until she can cope again. The NHS? Perhaps it should stand for 'No to Hip Sufferers'.

❧ Saturday 21 May

Conducting a marriage service must be like riding a bike because, despite my lack of practice, today's wedding of Katie and Ian proves a relaxed, joyous occasion. A few guests are held up by the Otley Show traffic, so the service starts 15 minutes late, but does it matter when the bride looks so lovely in her strapless ivory dress with veil and a heartdrop bouquet including roses and lilies?

Chanting by the choir during the signing of the register inhibits chatting at this 'natural break' – and in case anyone has forgotten, the Order of Service underlines that they should 'please be seated quietly'! As the newly-weds leave church, I resolve to avoid one particular adjective in describing Katie – in the past, brides who were called 'fetching' often ended up doing just that!

❧ Sunday 22 May

Our Christian Aid envelopes have been opened, and the result is splendid – £2,063.63, against £1,440.02 last year. The Ilkley total is £8,666.93 (£7,034.57) – a most encouraging result in a small town.

Today is Trinity Sunday, the start of the longest season of the Christian calendar, extending until our new year begins on Advent Sunday, which this year falls on 27 November. Trinity includes the summer holiday season, and can be rather routine, but there's rarely a dull moment when you're in the company not just of angels and archangels but Fr Alan Millar, one of our retired clergymen.

We're driving to Holy Trinity, Shaw, near Oldham, for the last service before they move into the hall while the church's leaking roof is repaired. Strange – we are doing almost the opposite! The incumbent, Richard Watson, was curate to Alan when he was Vicar of Cayton with Eastfield, Scarborough, between 1972 and 1988. Richard is today's celebrant, while Alan and I are among nine concelebrants!

Alan, who was born in Middlesbrough, served on a Royal Navy frigate in the Atlantic convoys from 1944 to 1946, working as a coder and completing his education in the vernacular. He can be serious – as when suggesting our congregation join him and his wife Jean in tithing – but has a terrific sense of humour. One of his best tales concerns three male parishioners at Middlesbrough who went to the pub after attending his confirmation class. When an attractive buxom blonde walked by, one confirmand exclaimed 'Phwoar!' 'You shouldn't do that – it's sinful!' said another, and the third agreed. Next week the matter was raised with Alan, who vindicated the blonde's admirer. 'To *look* is temptation,' he ruled. 'To *follow* is sin.'

♣ Monday 23 May

St Margaret's is supporting some young Christians overseas – quite literally. Nearly 130 tubular steel-framed chairs from the former hall are to be taken to Huddersfield to be put in a container leaving for Malawi. They will go to a church school in the Upper Shire Diocese, under arrangements made through the Christian African Relief Trust. Bryan Anson says: 'The 127 chairs were not sufficient for the new hall, and we were not able to match them with new ones.'

❧ *Tuesday 24 May*

It's election time again. New MPs so soon? No – fortunately this is only the first meeting of the new Otley Deanery Synod, which involves elections for representatives of both the clergy and laity. I resist any blandishments in my direction. I've had more than enough of that, and it's nice to sit on the back row and let it all go on around me!

A talk on 'The Church and the Environment' encourages us to become more ecologically friendly. In view of the large number of churches in Britain, Christians could make a significant green contribution, so I shall raise the matter with the PCC.

❧ *Wednesday 25 May*

Tonight sees one of the greatest come-backs in soccer history, when Liverpool battle back from 3–0 down at half-time to win the European championship on penalties. Having served my curacy in Liverpool, I'm delighted for the club and city.

Some unlucky Liverpool fans leave at half-time, convinced that all is lost. I miss the second half, the penalties, and even the first half – I'm not a football fan, although I did watch Bishopthorpe occasionally when I was at York. I also agreed to be patron of the bowls club, but somehow always had a prior engagement when they were at home.

❧ *Thursday 26 May*
CORPUS CHRISTI

One of the mysteries of divine providence is that God uses ordinary, everyday things to bring healing in a broken world.

Many centuries before Christ, Naaman, commander-in-chief of the King of Syria's army, expected that Elisha, the 'man of God', would do something spectacular to cure his leprosy. Instead, Elisha told him merely to bathe seven times in the River Jordan. Similarly, the first step in the Christian pilgrimage comes through baptism, in which ordinary water made special through blessing begins the internal cleansing of the personality – a lifelong process – by the Holy Spirit.

Today is Corpus Christi ('body of Christ' [Latin]), when we give thanks for Holy Communion, God's channel of grace via consecrated bread and wine. While bread is a basic human foodstuff, wine is more often a drink for celebrations. Its part in Communion recalls not only the blood shed by Christ on Calvary but anticipates the joy of Heaven, which Jesus depicted as a banquet. After handing round the cup of wine at the Last Supper, the Lord said: 'I will never again drink of the fruit of the vine until that day when I drink it new in the kingdom of God' (Mark 14:25).

This evening's celebration speaks to us of the destiny for which each of us was created – to be caught up in the life and love of God for ever. Holy Communion assures us that the risen Lord will be with us always. His Real Presence is with us, within us, as we celebrate this and every Eucharist.

❧ Friday 27 May

What's in a name? (*Romeo and Juliet*)

I have been lucky in having a surname which is so apt for a clergyman. I wonder what my old student Robert Tickle makes of his?

Robert trained at St Stephen's House, Oxford, when I was Principal, becoming curate of St Alban's, Hull. One fateful day, he wrote an article in his parish magazine saying that Christians should sometimes risk appearing foolish in their outreach to others. He could never have dreamed what would happen within days.

The article was noted by Hugh, then a reporter on the *Hull Daily Mail*, who persuaded Ken Dodd to donate a signed tickling-stick. Accompanied by a photographer, the pair set out on a tickling tour of the parish. Fr Tickle tickled shoppers, mums returning from school with their children ... anything that moved. The curate must have seemed a strange sight with his tickling-stick and biretta (a priest's square hat, not the gun made famous by James Bond). The *Hull Daily Mail* photographer certainly found a new angle – 45 degrees into the armpit!

Having spent most of his ministry in education, Robert is now Chaplain and Head of Religious Studies at an independent school in the Midlands. His students are fortunate to have such a fine role model in 'Mr T' – someone with a remarkable sense of humour who is not afraid to stand up for his beliefs.

Robert and Hugh have recently been invited to meet Ken Dodd at his Happiness Show at Bradford this Christmas. As an honorary Liverpudlian, I was asked too, but sadly have had to decline – I will be far too busy.

Despite my admiration for Fr Tickle, one thing worries me slightly – his memory, which is clearly not what it was. He tells a story of how he called on me at St Stephen's and I supposedly poured out two whiskies. He goes on:

> I asked Dr Hope if I could have water in mine, and he replied, 'No, you can't – get it down you, you lily-livered Southerner.'

Obviously, he has mixed me up with someone else.

✂ *Sunday 29 May*

The circus is in town, with all the fun of elephants, bears, kangaroos and crocodiles.

No, this is not entertainment from Billy Smart, but Fr Alan Brown, who is teaching us the 'state-of-the-ark' children's hymn, 'If I were a butterfly' with a little help from Fr Bernard and John Sunderland, our head server. It begins:

> If I were a butterfly
> I'd thank you, Lord, for giving me wings …

After reflecting on life as a robin and a fish in the sea ('I'd wiggle my tail and I'd giggle with glee'), verse two (with appropriate trunk-waving gestures) runs:

> If I were an elephant
> I'd thank you, Lord, by raising my trunk,
> and if I were a kangaroo
> you know I'd hop right up to you,
> and if I were an octopus
> I'd thank you, Lord, for my fine looks,
> but I just thank you, Father, for making me me.

Q: How do you know most fishes go to public schools?
A: Because many of them are eaten.

Our Family Service leaders believe in meeting the young 'where they are', which means that actions at the Family Service often speak at least as loudly as words. The 'old crocs' have a whale of a time with their animal antics, but I'm thankful to be at the back of the church where I can't be press-ganged to join in! Not surprisingly, the kids love it.

Providing some excellent backing are: Ian Bramley (piano), John's Dutch wife Corrie (guitar), and Nadine (cello), with Adrian Williams and his 14-year-old daughter Hermione (violins). Richard Williams (13) is laughing with (or at?) his sister, who is giggling at the words:

... if I were a fuzzy wuzzy bear,
I'd thank you, Lord, for my fuzzy wuzzy hair.

Hermione and some of her friends on the bus to Bradford Girls High School have recently had some good-natured fun serenading a colleague who really has 'fuzzy wuzzy hair'! Lucky lass – I could do with some of that myself.

At all today's services I mention that next Sunday I am to lay the foundation stone for our new parish hall, and St Margaret's expects that everyone – not just me! – will pray powerfully for fine weather. Two more baptisms after the main service. We're currently having a large number – five in May. Sometimes, like buses, they all come along at once.

❧ *Monday 30 May*

I remember, I remember,
the house where I was born ... (Thomas Hood)

Well, I don't, because I arrived in a nursing home in Sandal, Wakefield, but I do recall the house to which I was taken soon afterwards and where I lived until my late teens. It is 141 Thornes Lane, Wakefield.

Today is Bank Holiday, and I'm outside 141 for the filming of *My Yorkshire* for Yorkshire Television. Sadly my old home doesn't look as it did, having (like a former occupant) suffered through the passage of time. I am relieved to move on to Wakefield Cathedral, where I used to sing as a choirboy. If you imagine that being filmed for TV must be exciting, forget it – it's plain *boring*! 'Walk towards the camera, please ... now walk away ... move to the side ...' There's so much hanging around. We arrive at the cathedral this morning around 11 am, and are not to get away until 2 pm, by which time I really need a cup of tea.

Suddenly a chance meeting dispels my grumpiness and the day becomes worthwhile after all. A family come into the cathedral looking forlorn – indeed, lost. They are husband and wife (or partners) with a boy of 12 or 13. They come up to me and say: 'Can we light a candle, please, Vicar?' 'Of course!', I reply, and accompany them to the Candle Tree. I ask why they are here; it turns out their daughter was on drugs and died a year ago. They tell me her Christian name, and we hold hands and pray. I'm glad to have been of help, because I sense that lighting the candle met their spiritual needs. This was a simple gesture – a moment when actions spoke louder than words.

♣ *Tuesday 31 May*

> I should have known better with a girl like Ruth,
> than tell the-whole-and-nothing-but truth.

Because now, thanks to Miss Gledhill (6 March), those in any kind of business connected with cars or trains apparently look on me like the goose which laid the golden egg.

Today I'm temporarily living not in a yellow submarine but a yellow banana, the nickname for Network Rail's new measurement train (NMT), which uses hi-tech equipment to record the state of the track, to help in improving safety on the railways. Come to think of it, the Beatles' submarine could have been named *Banana*, because if you come up too quickly while under water you can develop the bends.

The NMT leaves Leeds at 10 am and travels via Doncaster and Sheffield, arriving in Derby around 12.30 pm. To keep everyone interested, there's an audio-visual presentation in rather technical language. Network Rail, the 'not for dividends' successor to Railtrack, hopes the increased data flow from the yellow banana will enable a shift from 'react and repair' to 'predict and prevent'. After years of public disquiet about safety on the railways, what reassures me about Network Rail is that it's a company limited by guarantee, with members instead of shareholders. Any operating profit is reinvested in the rail network, removing the temptation to put profits before people.

❧ SUMMER –

Standing with Today's Crucified

June

Wednesday 1 June

Journalists are rather like apes feeding off each others' backs. Sometimes a TV station will 'follow up' (i.e. pinch) a story in one of the broadsheets; at others, a broadsheet will 'get a new angle' on a tabloid's tale. What we are presented with as news is not always what it seems.

This morning Sky TV send a camera and sound man to the vicarage so I can be interviewed via a live link from London – was their interest kindled by Steve's and Jesus' work in *The Times*? There are two nine-minute slots starting at 10.30 am, with much hanging round before and between. The whole business takes about an hour.

I like watching the news and documentaries, but although I can receive BBC1, BBC2, ITV and Channel 4, like many people in Ilkley I can't get Channel 5 and Classic FM. My reception is worse than average, due to the number of trees surrounding the vicarage and its position beneath Ilkley Moor.

I took out a subscription to Sky on arriving here, but half the time the reception is poor, so at the end of the quarter I shall cancel it.

Friday 3 June

It's not a case of 'trouble at t'mill' tonight, but 'trouble wi' t'millin".

The invitation to the twenty-fifth Yorkshire Society dinner

plainly says 7.30 pm for 8 pm, but it's 8.30 pm before everyone is seated (or 'is sat', as many say around here). It's not the
fault of the Craiglands Hotel staff – people are just wandering around windbagging with no apparent sense of time. You
wouldn't get this at a big dinner in London.

There's a break after the food, and they're at it again –
'Blah! Blah! Did you know? Blah!' I'm here to speak for my
supper (they wouldn't care for my singing) but it's past my
bedtime – 11.05 pm – before I am introduced, so I am pretty
fed up (even if I present a graceful countenance). I crack a
few jokes, make a few points and sit down again.

Perhaps on occasions like this there should be a surcharge
at the end of the evening, depending on how long the meal
has gone beyond schedule due to excessive chit-chat. Or
perhaps not. I am reminded of the housemaster at a top
Yorkshire public school who was trying to coax into conversation a boy more interested in pork than talk. After several
vain attempts, and knowing the boy was a keen angler, he said:
'I understand you enjoy fishing, David. Tell me – what do you
use for bait?' The lad looked up for a moment, muttered
'Worms!' and went back to tackling the crackling. Maybe he
became a lighthouse-keeper.

❧ Saturday 4 June

I wonder how the *Yorkshire Post* weekend magazine has presented an interview which I gave to Michael Brown last
Friday?

Yes, there's some fine photos by Jim Moran, very readable
copy from Michael and ... oh dear, he has called Pam
Hearnshaw an 'elderly' member of the congregation but
referred to me only as the 'new' vicar'! No doubt due to production problems, the YP has omitted to give Michael his
proper title, 'Middle-Middle-Aged Religious Affairs

Correspondent', even though like me, I understand, he is about eligible to join the Boys of the Bus-Pass Brigade.

As Queen Victoria often was before she lost *her* husband, Pam is highly amused.

✆ *Sunday 5 June*

Ilkley Gazette photographer Adrian Murray is looking a little worried.

It's 9.50 am, and at 10 am I am to lay the foundation stone of our new parish hall – but there's not a trowel in sight for inclusion on the photos. As Adrian hunts for any tools which the building workers may have left around, retired clergyman Fr Peter Grierson is recalling a similar occasion he once attended. 'It certainly was a powerful sermon,' he says. 'The speaker seemed to look at everyone in turn before starting: "We are all part of Christ's Church, but are YOU going to be like pillars, holding it up – or caterpillars, which crawl in and out of a building?"' I bet that went down like a ton of bricks! Adrian need not be anxious, for I have a special trowel – a silver one more than a century old which was presented to F. S. Powell MP, to mark his laying the cornerstone of the parish room and Sunday School at St Margaret's on 16 November 1889.

Church members have been praying for fine weather, following my request last Sunday, but some are of little faith – in particular three members of the choir who turn up with umbrellas! The doubters are routed when only seconds before the stroke of ten a cloud rolls back and the sun breaks through.

After a hymn and lesson praising Christ, the cornerstone of the universal Church, churchwardens Barbara France and John Baggaley invite me to bless and lay the stone. Drops of water start to descend, but this is holy water, which I am daubing on to the stone with gusto. Although my name is on the plaque, the star of the show (especially with the ladies) is seven-year-old Ethan Atkinson, who is assisting his grandfather Steven Bainbridge as a server.

The stone is lifted into place by John Harrison, a partner and great-grandson of the founder of our builders, Enoch Harrison and Son Ltd, of Cononley, near Keighley. It only remains for me to say: 'I declare this foundation stone well and truly laid – in the name of the Father, the Son and the Holy Spirit!' I pray for everyone involved in the hall's construction, asking God to strengthen our family life and help us to spread the good news of God's love in Jesus. By 10.30 am, when the main service begins, the sun is back in bed. At 11.10 am, the heavens open, and it pours down all morning.

Today is the anniversary of my ordination as a priest in 1966 at Liverpool Cathedral by Bishop Stuart Blanch, later to become my predecessor as Archbishop of York. He was natural and relaxed, while I was both excited and humbled. In the evening, I celebrated High Mass at St John's, Tuebrook, for the first time, with my family present. It was a splendid, uplifting service. Having spent a year as a deacon, I was totally realistic, knowing exactly what was involved in being a priest. Perhaps best of all – and how many people today can say this? – I was content.

❧ Monday 6 June

Today I'm at a hundredth birthday party as I join in the centenary celebrations of All Saints' Mothers' Union, Ilkley. It's also the Otley Deanery Festival, and All Saints member Pauline Smith leads in a large number of distinctive banners and smiling faces.

The press enjoys categorising the MU – like the WI – as an organisation of tea-swilling, jam-making middle-class women with nothing better to do. In fact, the MU is an international movement doing a huge amount of good. For example, UK members help in contact centres and parent-and-toddler groups, and work with families affected by imprisonment, while the hugely successful 'Away from It All' scheme gives families under stress a much-needed holiday. Overseas, the MU is involved in orphanages, HIV/AIDS awareness-raising and healthcare.

In a society where far too many youngsters spend hours watching TV or surfing the internet alone in their bedrooms, the MU's upholding of family life based on Christian marriage has my full backing. Since the 1970s, men have been eligible to join this splendid organisation. But so far, I haven't been tempted.

❧ *Tuesday 7 June*

Down to London – I prefer it to 'up' – by train to see Black Rod (Lieut-General Sir Michael Willcocks) and the Clerk of the Parliaments (Paul Hayter) to discuss the arrangements for my introduction to the House of Lords in a fortnight. 'Introduction' is perhaps not quite the word, as I have been presented there three times already as Bishop of Wakefield, Bishop of London and Archbishop of York; this fourth occasion must be some kind of record. I have met Paul previously but not Sir Michael.

As usual, I am given the pass which gets you everywhere. Must remember to send in my expenses claim for the rail journey.

❧ *Wednesday 8 June*

This morning a group of clergymen and their wives from the Tamworth area visit St Margaret's. After coffee, I give a talk and we chat about church issues before finishing with prayer. Then it's back to the vicarage, where Barbara France and Anne Kilvington produce home-made soup and one of Ilkley's many attractions – herb and cheese bread from Betty's!

Perhaps we should consider welcoming visitors from other churches – especially in busy urban areas – when our new hall is open. Ilkley is charming and surrounded by beautiful scenery, with the moor to the south and Dales to the north. The reference in Psalm 23 to 'pastures green' might have been penned with us in mind. Around here they call Yorkshire 'God's own country'.

✖ *Saturday 11 June*

While I was Archbishop, the headmistress of a primary school I was visiting in Cumbria asked me to don my bishop's gear to show to the youngsters. I felt a right 'nana putting it on out of context, and the kids' eyes opened wide when I arrived – I must have looked like something out of *Star Wars*. One little boy was looking intently below the mitre, at my head. He raised his hand and asked thoughtfully: 'Please, sir – do you use hair-gel?' The best I could reply was: 'Certainly not! I use Yorkshire water – it's cheaper and better.'

All good fun, of course, but then another lad asked: 'Please sir – what happens when you die?' Apparently his mother had passed away a few months previously and he needed someone to make sense of his personal calamity. I said that his mum had loved him, he had loved her, and I was sure love was something that lasted for ever. I wish I could have got across that God was absolute Love and, like us, was a kind of person (rather than a Force or some kind of Big Brother). Maybe that would have been over his head and all he needed at that moment was to appreciate my conviction that his mum was safe.

You get a different view of things when you're in the bishop's chair. Sometimes, when I've been up at the front like a beached whale, I've looked at the faces before me and thought: 'What a bunch of "miserable sinners"! I know they're awake and attentive, but it looks as though they're going to *a wake*. Where is the joy that so marked out the first Christians?'

Today about 50 of my current (mainly cheerful) flock are with me at the Clarke-Foley Day Centre for a five-hour parish mission day, discussing how St Margaret's can reach out into the community, especially to the lonely. There are so many people out there spending hours on the internet searching – if they knew it – for spiritual direction and meaning, which they are unlikely to find in Harry Potter, *The Lord of the Rings* or *The Hitchhiker's Guide to the Galaxy*.

Appropriately, it is St Barnabas' Day. Barnabas means 'son of encouragement', and the Acts of the Apostles depicts him as someone positive – always kind and often 'opening doors' for others. When the early Church was strapped for cash, he sold an estate and gave the proceeds to the apostles (Acts 4:32–37). How many of us today would do anything remotely similar, I wonder? The Church's first priority should not be to aim for 'bums on seats' and 'pounds on the plate'. But if through helping others we let them glimpse something of the love of Christ, who shared our joys and bore our griefs, sometimes the other things may perhaps follow too.

Everyone agrees the new parish hall will give us opportunities to become more outward-looking. Another meeting is to be held in the autumn, by which time, hopefully, ideas put forward today should have gelled into an action plan.

❧ Sunday 12 June

Sometimes during a Sunday service we are given a glimpse of glory, as three of Jesus' disciples experienced at the

Transfiguration (Mark 9:2–8). Such a moment occurs today while people are going up to receive Holy Communion.

Following her recent hip operation, Pam Hearnshaw stayed in her seat last week for the Sacrament to be brought to her. But today she decides to walk to the altar with a stick. As she moves into the aisle, she falters slightly. To her great surprise, Trevor takes her arm and helps her up to the Communion rail. 'He hasn't done that for three years – something just clicked,' she says afterwards.

In a sermon on faith and doubt, Fr Bernard says faith is not something removed from our normal experience since we take so much on trust every day – *usually* without mishaps:

> 'You didn't check your chair before you sat down this morning, did you? Neither did someone at the Probus Club the other day – and it collapsed beneath him.'

Another meal at the Craiglands Hotel – this time an eightieth birthday lunch for parishioner Gerald Hodges, former treasurer of Ilkley Urban District Council and director of finance with Bradford Metropolitan District Council, who was Bradford University's treasurer from 1986 to 1997. Among the guests is the university's chancellor, Baroness Betty Lockwood, with whom I chat during the meal.

The speeches are going well when at 3.30 pm there is a late arrival – Fr Alan Brown, who has just finished conducting a baptism. Is he pondering the fate of the five foolish virgins (Matthew 25:1–13), who were also *en retard* ? By this time, most of the food has been removed. In similar circumstances our friend Maria Theresa might have observed: 'Let him eat cake.' Fortunately for Alan, there is still some coffee in which to dunk his *gâteau* – although this well-bred man wouldn't dream of it!

❧ *Monday 13 June*

You have to admire St Paul, if you study his letters and the Acts of the Apostles, because despite his many achievements he was acutely aware at times of his human frailty, but carried on preaching. He confessed to the church at Corinth (1 Corinthians 2:3f):

> ... I came to you in weakness and in fear and in much trembling. My speech and my proclamation were not with plausible words of wisdom, but with a demonstration of the Spirit ...

I know (at least in part) how Paul felt! Forty years ago today, I was ordained deacon at St Chad's, Kirkby, Liverpool, by Lawrence Brown, Bishop of Warrington, who later became Bishop of Birmingham. I had considerable feelings of trepidation about what might lie ahead, and was conscious of needing the grace and gifts of the Holy Spirit. It was such a relief to feel surrounded and supported by the prayers of the congregation. Perhaps my words will encourage someone today who is wondering about taking the same step – I do hope so!

❧ *Tuesday 14 June*

Tonight I ask the PCC to consider the Deanery Synod's call for churches to 'go green'. Our new hall will be environmentally friendly, and it's clear any new church lighting should be energy efficient. No resolutions are passed, but the issue is to be borne in mind from now on.

✢ *Wednesday 15 June*

About a week ago Jasper Gerard, of the *Sunday Times,* rang up
to see if I'd answer some questions for an article for the paper's
motoring section. I've turned down a lot of journalists
recently, and wasn't sure about motoring writers – give 'em
an inch, I thought, and they'll take an L-plate. However, Jasper
was persuasive (was he once a second-hand car dealer?) so I
agreed and we chatted for a while. He then asked if I'd mind
being photographed on Ilkley Moor in my Land Rover
Freelander. It would take 'about half an hour'. Pull the other
one, I thought, but agreed. In fact, the process takes around 90
minutes.

This morning a Lotus supplied by Yorkshire-based special-
ist car dealer JCT 600 turns up at the vicarage. How Jasper
pulled it off, I don't know – like the Holy Trinity, it's a mystery beyond all telling. Off we glide towards the church,
where I get into my cassock and cotta [shortened surplice] for
the first set of photos. Not wishing to look like a motor show
sex siren, I refuse to sit on the bonnet. As usual it's a case of,
'Thanks – now move to the other side – a bit to the right …'
Up we go along Wells Road with Rombalds Hotel on the left
and the vicarage on the right. Beyond the cattle grid, acres of
moorland stretch into the distance. As I drive, Jasper's photographer, Michael Powell, takes shots through the driving
mirror. The Naked Rambler hasn't been seen for a while, so
Michael gets coverage but misses any uncoverage.

I'm thinking of giving up (or at least cutting down on)
journalists next Lent – their attention encourages the sin of
pride, and they're time-consuming. Motoring writers are the
worst sort. Tell them, 'My tread is with angels', and they'll
only reply, 'But is it within the legal limit?'

❧ *Sunday 19 June*

The normally laid-back Alan Brown had rather a surprise in 1998 when an OAP turned up at Leeds University, where he is Senior Lecturer in the School of Healthcare, asking to be accepted on a postgraduate course in Healthcare Chaplaincy.

This was no ordinary mature student but 72-year-old Sister Liz – originally a nurse but now one of the Sisters of Notre Dame (Our Lady's Convent) at Kettering. The two-year course would involve her in private study back at the convent, but one day a month she would have to rise at 5 am for a return trip of 350-plus miles, arriving home around midnight.

In today's sermon Alan says:

> I asked Sister Liz what her Mother Superior thought about her coming on the course. She answered: 'Oh, I didn't ask her. She would never have allowed me to go to the interview!'

Before long, Mother Superior did give her blessing to this un-convent-ional nun's educational expeditions, and today Sister Liz MA is teaching spirituality in a hospice to nurses less than half her age.

Alan's point is that it's never too late to learn – but the best religious education is not for spiritual couch-potatoes. If Christians are to make any impact, they need to be 'thinking' people rather than empty vessels filled with pre-digested ideas. He wants the laity to participate actively in the 'learning-teaching' which we hope to introduce at St Margaret's.

❧ *Tuesday 21 June*

When you are being introduced at the House of Lords for the fourth time, you have to do it differently.

Having arrived at King's Cross around 11 am, I take the tube to Victoria and walk the half-mile or so to Parliament. As custom dictates, I provide lunch for my two sponsors – Lord Crathorne (Lord Lieutenant of North Yorkshire) and Lord Habgood (another former Archbishop of York) whom my spellchecker wants to call respectively, but not respectfully, *Lord Carthorse* and *Lord Haggard*. Also present are two friends and my nephew, Andrew. We have an enjoyable meal – smoked salmon and chicken mushed up in a mushroomy sauce, with a French white wine. My mobile is switched off, which makes the meal even more pleasant!

At 1.45 pm I'm off to robe and rehearse briefly in the Chamber. Former Education Secretary Estelle Morris is also being introduced and is with her sponsor, the brilliant film producer David Puttnam. Estelle is good company, and we chat for a while. Colin Bennetts, the Bishop of Coventry, says the prayers, and then the Estelle and David Show begins. David Puttnam may be thinking, 'Lights, cameras – action', but of course these proceedings won't be on telly. Estelle and I present our papers to the Clerk, swear the Oath of Allegiance, sign the roll, shake hands with Lord Falconer, the Lord Chancellor, then out we go. We disrobe quickly, returning as fully fledged members of the Lords.

It's about this point that David Puttnam probably starts thinking, '*The Road to Westminster* – take two'. Someone is beckoning at me, so I head towards them automatically, for-getting they're in the Conservative benches and I'm a cross-bencher. I'm about a yard away and about to sit down, when I'm whisked deftly away. My mistake causes a little *frisson* of excitement, and no doubt I'll get some poor reviews ('Hope's hopeless'; 'David's dreadful') when my peers arrive home.

There are no 'credits' in the little drama I have depicted other than to the House of Lords itself. Its members are dis-tinguished people from every walk of life, and it has more informed – sometimes heated – debate than that in the Commons. It is a restraining Chamber, which is especially important when the Government of the day has a huge majority. It can raise questions and revise legislation, although due to the Parliament Act it can no longer block legislation completely. Parish duties permitting, I hope be an 'extra' about once every five weeks.

❧ *Wednesday 22 June*

Many older readers will remember Garth, an early super-hero appearing in the *Daily Mirror* from 1943. I didn't often see him, since we took the *Yorkshire Post* at home, but when I did, I had to admire him. He was a huge brute of a man with rippling muscles.

So well known was Garth that he featured in 'The Spider', a song by Michael Flanders and Donald Swann, those post-war musical geniuses whose superb songs included tributes to the gnu ('the g-nicest work of g-nature in the zoo') and the rhinoceros with its 'bodger on the bonce'.

'The Spider' is a psychological drama featuring a man who has seen off grizzly bears, cobras and crocodiles but whose worst nightmare is to 'find that there's a spider in the bath' – a thought enough to make anyone scream. Half-way through the song occur the memorable lines:

> What a frightful looking beast –
> half an inch across at least –
> it would frighten even Superman or Garth.

Now I am not afraid of spiders, wasps, daddy long-legs or mice. What I *am* frightened of is those nasty, predatory speed cameras! I really need a Road Angel, the new wonder of the world, which bleeps to give you advance warning of them. I am seriously considering having one installed in my car.

Our Garth, Lay Reader Garth Kellett, is to be ordained at Bradford Cathedral on Sunday to serve as a non-stipendiary minister at St Margaret's for about 25 hours a week. Garth is a former civil servant who worked at the Ministry of Defence until his retirement. Physically, he does not resemble his super-hero namesake; he is short, like Zacchaeus, who deceived the public by extorting too much in tax from them until he met Jesus (Luke 19:1–10). Garth was frightened of spiders until he was about six. Now, he says, he would only be afraid of being 'shut up within myself' – but having been found by God he does not fear that possibility. Until 1986 Garth believed in God but thought 'he probably isn't interested in me'. His position was similar to that of the twentieth-century French mystic Simone Weil – in many ways a prophet for this generation. In her spiritual autobiography, *Waiting on God*, she wrote:

> As soon as I reached adolescence I saw the problem of God as a problem of which the data could not be obtained here below, and I decided that the only way of being sure not to reach a wrong solution ... was to leave it alone ... I neither affirmed not denied anything ...

But when she was 29, Simone came across George Herbert's poem 'Love', a description of Christ inviting those weary of self-centredness to 'taste my meat' – the consecrated bread and wine of Holy Communion:

> Love bade me welcome; yet my soul drew back,
> guiltie of dust and sinne.
> But quick-ey'd Love, observing me grow slack
> from my first entrance in,

> drew nearer to me, sweetly questioning
> if I lack'd any thing.
>
> 'A guest,' I answer'd, 'worthy to be here':
> Love said, 'You shall be he.'
> 'I, the unkind, ungrateful? Ah, my dear,
> I cannot look on Thee.'
> Love took my hand, and smiling did reply,
> 'Who made the eyes but I?'
>
> 'Truth Lord; but I have marr'd them: let my shame
> go where it doth deserve.'
> 'And know you not,' says Love, 'Who bore the blame?'
> 'My dear, then I will serve.'
> 'You must sit down,' says Love, 'and taste My meat'.
> So I did sit and eat.

Simone learnt the poem by heart, and said it repeatedly. Later, she wrote:

> I used to think I was merely reciting it as a beautiful poem, but without knowing it the recitation had the virtue of a prayer. It was during one of those recitations that … Christ himself came down and took possession of me. In all my arguments about the insolubility of the problem of God I had never foreseen the possibility of … a real contact, person to person, here below, between a human being and God.

In a similar way, 18 years ago (though perhaps less intensely), God 'got personal' for Garth. He realised 'just how selfish I was' and that 'something was expected of me'. His brave new step at the age of 64 – when most of his Civil Service contemporaries are ready to wind down – is being taken to 'tell of God's love for each of us and how we may respond to it'.

In case Beatles fans among you are wondering, despite his special age Garth is not yet losing his hair. He admits to be beyond staying out 'till quarter to three', but says Maggie is still needing him, or at least still feeding him!

✣ Thursday 23 June

Everyone knows that spinach is something which plain girls give to wimps about to have sand kicked in their faces – or worse. It's not something that tall, dark strangers offer to beautiful blondes at the start of something so big that it leads to wedding bells.

But that's precisely what happened when principal cellist Thomas Wharton met viola-player Vessela Gueorguieva and another East European girl as a member of the National Chamber Orchestra of South Africa in 1995. There was no point in singing 'Hi, Hi, Miss Bulgarian Pie', because Vessi and her friend hardly spoke a word of English. Thomas simply smiled and offered spinach pie, which they accepted – to his relief. It could only have happened in Mafikeng (now known as Mmbatu)! Thomas persevered ('We managed to find other means of communication'), and within two years he and Vessi were married, firstly at St Thomas', Stockport, where Thomas grew up, and then in Bulgaria with Vessi's family present 'to make doubly sure'. In 2000 the couple moved to Ilkley, and started worshipping at St Margaret's with Thomas' mother, Lay Reader Nadine Wharton.

Thomas was combining freelancing with the Hallé and other leading orchestras with teaching at Bradford Grammar School, but gradually felt guided towards ordination. He says: 'I fought against it to start with, but increasingly felt I wanted to hear and respond to God's call. I felt that if others recognised it, I was prepared to say, "Yes!"' Today, after rigorous training at Westcott House, Cambridge, Thomas (now 33) is on retreat waiting to be ordained on Sunday at Bradford. Next Tuesday he and Vessi, with their sons Anthony (eight) and Michael (three), are moving to Threshfield, North Yorkshire, where Thomas starts work as an assistant curate at St Michael and All Angels, Linton.

Thomas says is excited by the appointment of Uganda-born Bishop of Birmingham Dr John Sentamu as the next Archbishop of York. Having found a 'sense of belonging and sharing' in the multi-cultural church in South Africa, he hopes a new mood of optimism will ripple out with the arrival of a new 'rock' in the See. So do I!

Thomas would like to have time to keep up his cello-playing at Linton. I hope the new curate will – I'm told that few of those who heard him perform the Dvořák Cello Concerto with the Airedale Symphony Orchestra at Ilkley in 2003 will ever forget it.

🍀 *Friday 24 June*

Most of the morning is taken up with being filmed and interviewed for *My Yorkshire* at Flamborough Head.

My family used to go on holiday there every year during the first fortnight in August when I was five to 15 or so. My Dad, being a busy builder, spent weekends with us and returned home on Sunday nights. He seldom, if ever, took a whole week off but lived to be 80, as did my mother. Walking on the clifftops today, watching the sea birds massing, brings back a host of happy memories.

🍀 *Saturday 25 June*

Tonight, in aid of the hall appeal fund, the ladies have arranged a safari supper, an event for which everyone must be mobile since the courses are held in different venues. It's not recommended for those prone to dyspepsia! We meet in church for the starters, and end up at the vicarage, where there's an impressive display of puddings. You don't *christen* these, of course, but Anne Kilvington has given ours names like David's Delight, Hope's Heaven, Bishop's Best, Father's Fancy, Wakefield Wonder and Baron's Bliss. The ladies have been generous with the cream. Thornes Thunderbolt was withdrawn – that was the rhubarb crumble, which turned out to be apple. Anne said afterwards:

> I thought it would be fun to give them all a name connected with Fr David since we were invading the vicarage. He thought they sounded like entrants for the Ebor Handicap!

The participants in the safari supper have gained a few pounds – some on themselves, but St Margaret's Hall Appeal has 'put on' over £2,000! Advice to parishes thinking of having a similar evening:

> A safari supper's a fine event,
> But please remember – never in Lent!

❧ Sunday 26 June

God has ways of making you humble, as I am reminded on my way into Bradford Cathedral this morning for the Ordination of Deacons. I have just entered this small and friendly building when a member of the cathedral staff asks if I am going to be ordained.

Bradford Cathedral is a gem set against the run-down district of Little Germany, whose chief advantage for Yorkshire Christians is that parking near the cathedral is free early on

Sundays. I wonder if this helps to swell the cathedral's collections? There can be few places in Britain which remind people more of the possibility of sudden death than this cathedral. In front of the congregation this morning is a plaque commemorating the 56 people who died when fire ripped through Bradford City's Valley Parade ground on 11 May 1985. St Margaret's parishioner Gerald Hodges was one of three trustees overseeing the distribution of £4.25 million raised by an appeal for the bereaved and injured.

By coincidence, Bishop David James shares his name with the Manchester City and England goalkeeper. Both are in the business of saving – souls and goals respectively – and both are often to be found right underneath a cross.

The sermon is given by the Revd Dilly Baker, Warden of Scargill Retreat Centre, near Kettlewell, who has just taken a three-day retreat for the eight ordinands, two of whom are women. Dilly oozes enthusiasm and has everyone on the edge of their seats during her sermon. She begins with a story about a bedtime conversation she had with her son, then six.

> I popped in to kiss him goodnight.
>
> 'Mum, are you a Christian?' he asked me.
>
> 'Yes, I am – I try to follow the teachings of Jesus and be the sort of person he'd like me to be.'
>
> 'Um', came back the thoughtful but unconvinced response, 'Is Daddy a Christian?' 'Yes', I said, wondering where the interrogation was leading.
>
> 'Well, I'm not going to be one – when I grow up, I'm going to be a train driver.'

Dilly says Christians are not a set of unworldly saints but people who break bread together and then try to share 'the nourishment that Christ brings' with others. She goes on:

We are being asked to stand alongside those in whom Christ is still being crucified today. And some of you will be travelling, bleary-eyed, up to Edinburgh on Saturday at 5 am [for the Make Poverty History debt march] to stand in solidarity alongside those who are denied the good things of the Earth, who are still suffering in a world of plenty. Churches are not places of refuge from the suffering of the world. Rather we are to be a people who take seriously a crucified God, recognising in the cries and the struggles of those who suffer a God who is strangely present.'

The service is dominated by the charisma (with its original meaning of 'gifts of the Holy Spirit') of David James. Standing tall, broad and welcoming behind the altar, David is like a top-class goalie with safe hands catching the ball and feeding it out to his team. The love of God which he has caught exudes from him, with potential to travel far beyond Valley Parade, depending on the response of the ordinands and everyone else present.

Bishop David interviews two of the ordinands just before the 'kick-off'. Pam Coles says she is looking forward to ministering 'from the cradle to the grave' in Clayton, Bradford, while Thomas Wharton predicts he will be more nervous for his first time in the pulpit than before playing a cello solo. Afterwards, as the eight new reverends go outside into the sunshine for the official photos, Dilly tells inquirers her son's name is Theo (*'theos'* [Greek], 'a god'). 'Another man who thinks he is God,' she says, exuberant as ever.

❧ Tuesday 28 June

Among the heresies condemned by the early Church was docetism (*'dokeein'* [Greek], 'to seem') – the notion that Jesus *seemed* to have a physical body but in reality was a pure spirit and hence could not die physically. The belief was important to the Gnostics, who believed that because matter was evil God would not take a material body.

Two millennia later, Ilkley artist Leslie Simpson has avoided the artistic error of dog-etism in his painting for Fr Richard Hoyal of Ollie the Collie, which retired clergyman Graham Sanders and his wife Mary are taking down to Bristol today to mark Fr Richard's Silver Jubilee as a priest.

Leslie says: 'It was originally suggested that Ollie's head should be replaced by Richard's, but it would have looked like a man in a dog's suit so I re-drew the head as normal, adding a halo above it.' He breathes a sigh of relief at not having compromised the humanity – sorry, caninity – of Ollie. He adds: 'It would also have suggested that the clergy are dogs-bodies' – which of course all too often they are. As usual Ollie is strikingly slim, and his goggle eyes would scare off anyone (or thing) threatening the sheep.

Prayers are said for both Fr Richard and St Margaret's when the Mothers' Union attend Evensong at Liverpool's Anglican Cathedral today, after visiting the Roman Catholic 'Wigwam' Cathedral of Christ the King, where there is a display on the 1982 visit to Liverpool of Pope John Paul II. It's hot and sticky, and those MU members with their minds on lower things during Evensong enjoy watching the tiny probationer choristers scratching underneath their ruffs. I hope they don't 'get it in the neck' afterwards – as our ladies should for lack of attention!

❧ *Wednesday 29 June*

At All Saints' vicarage in Clifton, Bristol, Ollie is getting to know Richard and Muriel, who are thrilled with their personalised painting. They have also received a mini-sketch of

'Fr Richard the Collie' in a signed copy of Leslie's book. Richard says: 'At last I begin to suspect what fame may taste like!'

☙ Thursday 30 June

How often does anyone write – and receive – his or her own obituary? Has it ever happened? You tell me. The nearest equivalent I can think of is 'I told you I was ill,' inscribed (in Irish) on Spike Milligan's tombstone.

Today Richard Whiteley, OBE, presenter of *Countdown* and Mayor of Wetwang, gets the tribute he wanted when the *Ilkley Gazette* announces in four words which will go down in legend in Yorkshire and far beyond:

LOCAL FERRET MAN DIES

Speaking as a fair-minded Yorkshireman, I consider the headline on a par with that in the South Gloucestershire edition of the *Bristol Evening Post* which broke the news of the engagement of Prince Charles and Camilla Parker-Bowles with the headline:

TETBURY MAN TO WED

The *Gazette* says Richard will always be remembered for the night in 1977 when he was bitten by a ferret on Yorkshire Television's programme *Calendar*. 'I shall be known as the ferret man when I die,' he told the *Gazette*. 'The *Ilkley Gazette* will have an obituary with the headline, "Local Ferret Man Dies".'

The genial *Countdown* host died on Sunday in Leeds General Infirmary. He had been admitted to Bradford Royal Infirmary in May after developing pneumonia. Richard lived in Burley Woodhead, only yards from Ilkley Moor. I met him several times at social or other charity functions. He was always relaxed, jolly and enthusiastic about life, with a great interest in people. He was a big man in every way.

The *Gazette* quotes Richard as having said 18 months ago that because he loved the Ilkley area so much, 'My next move will be to heaven.' In a sense he was part-way there while with us physically, for he had that sense of fun which was a hallmark of great Christians like Archbishop Michael Ramsey and Cardinal Basil Hume. According to St Symeon the New (949–1022) Christ is – amongst everything else – 'the gaiety and the mirth'. Maybe great characters like Richard Whiteley walk lightly in life, aware that troubles are passing but God's love is eternal. I wonder if the 'local ferret man' is already causing havoc in heaven?

July

When the great Jewish 'man of God' Elijah died, his prophet's mantle was taken up by Elisha. I have rather a soft spot for the latter. There's a strange story in 2 Kings 2 of how a group of boys got more than they bargained for when they jeered at him, 'Go away, baldhead!' He 'cursed them in the name of the Lord', and along came two she-bears which mauled 42 of the cheeky urchins (children at our Family Service, please note!). I rather feel for poor Elisha. Today he would have bought some hair-restorer or asked himself the question which every balding gent poses sometimes: 'Toupee or not toupee?'

I bet Elijah's mantle was nowhere near as bright and beautiful as any of the 186 jackets owned by Richard ('once-bitten, twice-nightly') Whiteley, whose ferret mantle has been taken up in Ilkley by Adrian Robinson, our verger. There are ferrets at the bottom of Adrian's garden in a cage big enough to let in plenty of fresh air: Adrian says if you aren't careful, ferrets can smell 'like a poke of devils'. His pair are both female – Tizwin, aged two, named after a rough Apache beverage, and Marlene, 'an inverted compliment to a friend'.

Adrian thinks Richard was unlucky to have been bitten. 'I have never been attacked by my ferrets, and neither have any of my visitors – yet,' he says. 'If you handle them properly, they trust you. The ferret which went for Richard must have been frightened by the TV lights or noise from onlookers.' No doubt, but I intend to give Tizwin and Marlene a pretty wide berth.

Adrian can do without any more injuries. In 1996 he was in a serious accident involving another motorbike. His right leg was badly injured, and he was on crutches for 11 months. He has had eight operations since the collision, and is due for what he hopes will be his last later this month. He has an obvious limp, and could not kick a football or jump off a wall. Despite all this, he will help anyone and everyone, and this self-confessed 'driven person' goes the extra mile in his cleaning and other duties in church. The ladies think he's lovely.

♣ *Saturday 2 July*

Ask not for whom the bell tolls – it tolls for the 30,000 children who, according to Oxfam, die every day somewhere in the world due to poverty.

As noon approaches today, more than 300 people are gathered in front of Ilkley's bandstand on The Grove. There's not a police officer in sight during the march, which begins at 11 am. The police were warned about the event, but decided they were needed elsewhere – all everyone is expecting in sedate Ilkley is another outbreak of middle-class politeness.

It's good to see many teenagers among the protesters. They include a group of girls from Ilkley Grammar School with a flag displaying 56 African flags. Some people carry large yellow Fairtrade plastic bananas. Others have placards with slogans such as 'Cancel Third World Debt' and 'Stand up for Africa'. Ironically, across The Grove is a more familiar Saturday-morning sign:

> ILKLEY MARKET
> THE FRESHEST
> TASTIEST
> EGGS YOU WILL
> EVER BUY!!!
> LAID YESTERDAY

No one thinks of throwing an egg at local MP Ann Cryer, newly elected on to the Parliamentary Committee of the Parliamentary Labour Party. Last Wednesday she told Tony Blair that her stepdaughter-in-law Elizabeth grew up in Kenya, where many sugar-growers have been bankrupted due to the EC's subsidising of European sugar beet. So many small cane-producers in the Ngerie area have lost their livelihoods that the sugar refinery has closed. What Africa needs above all, Ann tells today's crowd, is fair trade. I recall 20 years ago meeting a woman in Ghana who used to walk nine miles, three times a week, to collect half a bucket of muddy water. Another memory is the shock of seeing children pick through rubbish heaps for scraps of bread and chicken bones.

Just before noon, the TV crews ask people carrying individual letters of the alphabet to move away from the bandstand so their message can be seen on screen:

M-A-K-E   P-O-V-E-R-T-Y   H-I-S-T-O-R-Y

Then a drum beats every three seconds for a minute and 20 red balloons are released to remind people of all those dying children. Much of England expects a good deal from the G8 leaders meeting at Gleneagles Hotel in Scotland on Wednesday.

The day is not over for Ann. After lunch she's off to nearby Keighley for more exercise – and another speech – on the Keighley Inter-Faith Group's annual Walk for Friendship. The 170 or so walkers stop first at the Medina Mosque, where Faisal Iqbal (11) recites from the Koran and Maths teacher Arafat Latif explains that Islam means 'peace'. He says Muslims regard both Moses and Jesus as prophets, and consider it sinful to speak disrespectfully of them. Further on, at St Anne's Roman Catholic Church, several young Muslim children are wondering what the font is all about. They are surprised to learn that it's for daubing holy water on to foreheads rather than pouring water on to feet!

Muslims are expected to pray five times a day – not easy at any time, but especially hard in summer. Their prayer schedule depends on the amount of daylight, and around the longest day prayers can begin at 4 am and finish at 11 pm! Prayer is better than sleep? Try telling that to many Anglicans!

✿ *Sunday 3 July*

There's been almost saturation coverage in the media of the coming G8 summit. Will there be a new deal for Africa and the developing world, or will the national (self-) interest be the first consideration (as usual)?

Christian Kam, from Cameroon, an IT student who is a server at St Margaret's, symbolises the huge, untapped potential of Africa. Aged 34, he is broad and over 6 ft tall, strong, courteous and willing to help. Christian is worried that after all the noise about Africa, little will change next week. He detects a growing public desire for fairer world trade but, like Chancellor Gordon Brown, fears that making poverty history will prove a lifetime's work.

St Margaret's parishioners Maggie Kellett and Jan Bramley were among 100,000 people involved in a minute's silence yesterday on The Meadows, Edinburgh. Maggie says: 'There was a countdown, then total silence – this was a most powerful way of showing our feelings.'

It is good that they were able to go – sometimes, faith simply has to be expressed in action. As the Letter of James asks us:

> If a brother or sister is naked and lacks daily food, and one of you says to them, 'Go in peace; keep warm and eat your fill', and yet you do not supply their bodily

needs, what is the good of that? (James 2:15–16)

Choir member Stephen Murdoch, who leads the prayers today, has taken to heart words by Archbishop Rowan Williams:

> We need to be more angry about the situation than we are. The fact of 30,000 avoidable deaths every day is something which ought to be intolerable for us to live with.

Instead of the usual response, 'Hear our prayer', Stephen asks us to reply: '*N'kosi sikeleli Afrika*' ('God bless Africa'). He complains to God about 'poor countries suffering from widespread corruption, caused both by exterior interests and the greed of dishonest politicians'.

There is some truth in that, but to me it's not the whole story – perhaps the real trouble is that the picture is simply too big for the politicians to cope with. Gordon Brown, for example, is manifestly committed to the developing world but even he can't keep his finger on the pulse all the time. After all the hype which precedes top-level meetings between world leaders over poverty, it's easy for politicians to pass resolutions, but ensuring the delivery of pledges at local level is a different matter – especially once the television cameras have gone away. Perhaps the greatest temptation facing Government ministers who profess a desire to 'make poverty history' is to look only as far as the next General Election.

✣ *Thursday 7 July*

A day that I shall not forget – but, sadly, for all the wrong reasons.

Before mid-morning, a friend rings from London. He has

been on the internet, and says news is breaking of a terrorist atrocity in central London with many casualties feared. Immediately my mind goes back to 1993, when I was Bishop of London. On 24 April from my office I heard the dull thud of what turned out to be an IRA bomb exploding in Bishopsgate, a considerable distance away. The blast killed one and injured more than 40 people.

When my friend has rung off, I go on the internet myself, and learn that the news is indeed grim. At 8.50 am, within 50 seconds, three bombs exploded on underground trains just outside Liverpool Street and Edgware Road stations, and on another travelling between King's Cross and Russell Square. Almost an hour later, a fourth bomb blast occurred on a double-decker bus in Tavistock Square, not far from King's Cross. The four suicide bombers have murdered several dozen innocent people, in the process causing chaos for millions of commuters.

Ever since the Bishopsgate bomb, I have feared that something like this would happen. Now that it has, I feel helpless in the face of the enormity of the event and the horrific experiences of those caught up in it. It has opened our eyes once again to the manifestation of sheer evil in human hearts, and the fact that a few religious zealots are prepared to destroy others' lives in pursuit of their misguided ends. I recall a remark by the Chief Rabbi that religion is like the weather – sometimes good, but at times very bad indeed. Now, at this moment of national crisis, all I can do is commend the bereaved and their families to God ('Help of the helpless', as 'Abide with Me' puts it), not forgetting to pray for the Government and those in the emergency and security services.

❧ Friday 8 July

The start of the quiet summer period – in Ilkley, at least – gives me a chance to give credit to our church choir, among the best for its size (16 at full strength) in the country. When Channel 4 gets round to *100 Best Choirs* after *100 Best Laundrettes* and *100 Best Dry-Stone Wallers*, ours will surely be worth including. Admittedly, they are helped by the wonderful acoustics in St Margaret's, but sometimes (especially during the Sanctus, Benedictus and Agnus Dei of the Sung Eucharist) you could echo the words of Jacob at Bethel:

> 'This is none other than the house of God, and this is the gate of heaven.' (Genesis 28:17)

I say this to put into perspective a 'cards on the table' meeting with the choir to relay back comments about our music made at the parish mission day. Only one chorister had been present, and some of the others seem have gained the impression (not from her) that I want to reduce dramatically the choir's part in the services. Not at all; I am merely seeking what the Collect for Pentecost calls 'a right judgement in all things'. My point was that music should serve the liturgy, not the other way round. No personal criticisms were intended, and I hope no one feels any.

Sometimes I feel an essential criterion for entry to the Diplomatic Service should be previous experience as a Church of England clergyman.

❧ Sunday 10 July

The General Synod is well under way at York, and for me being in Ilkley is a merciful deliverance.

Until I started this diary entry, I'd hardly given it a second

Artist Graeme Willson with Archbishop David at the dedication of *The Madonna of the Moors*. (*Ilkley Gazette*)

With Muriel Hoyal and Fr Richard at the dedication of the new parish hall. (*Ilkley Gazette*)

Town Crier Chris Richards with Ilkley TIC Manager Peter Bailey and Richard Whiteley. *(Ilkley Gazette)*

Philippa 'Hatwoman' Higgins on 'Ilkla Moor wi' t' at'!

Teresa Cannell, Fr Alan Millar and Canon Bernard Gribbin, crossing the Wharfe.

Reader Catherine Gibson and Honorary Curate Fr Garth Kellett.

Verger Adrian Robinson gives a lesson in ferret-handling to Honorary Assistant Priest Fr Alan Brown.

James and Alexandra Keeley with mutual friend Charlie.

Lay Reader Nadine Wharton with *Twinkletoes* members: Gina Williams, Hollie Johnson, Helena Beeson and Jenny Dybeck.

Another victim for Fr Tickle. (*Hull Daily Mail*)

(Victor de) Jesus. (© Nigel Hillier)

A cookery lesson for Sarah Williams from Hermione and Richard.

With proud father Philip Allen at the baptism of 'miracle' baby Louis.

The Church of tomorrow: Helena Beeson, Richard and Hermione Williams and Mathilda Conversy.

Fr David with Hugh Little.

Fr David with David James, Bishop of Bradford. (*Ilkley Gazette*)

thought, but now I can just imagine Synod members discussing women bishops and getting excited about the issue. On these occasions you can always predict who will say what, and the poor Archbishops have to sit from morning until night listening to it all.

The word 'Synod' comes from the Greek words '*syn*', 'together', and '*hodos*', 'a way' – 'travelling together', you might put it. Unfortunately, the Church of England's governing body is modelled too much on the House of Commons where, instead of being asked to decide, the Members are called on to divide ('Has Christ been divided?' – 1 Corinthians 1:13). The media love the adversarial system which Anglicanism has allowed itself to be talked into. They like our 'jaw-jaw' to resemble 'war-war', and do what they can to encourage this.

I should prefer to see a looser kind of assembly usually operating without votes (after all, the early Church operated through councils aiming for consensus) and more matters being discussed at local level. No one can be sure whether the present demands for change on issues like the ordination of women and homosexual clergy are in accordance with the 'mind of Christ' or merely the result of yielding to secular pressure – possibly temporary – for anti-discrimination measures. The current restless period does not faze me unduly, however much I may disagree with many of the proposals of the reformers. I accept the wisdom of the 'Gamaliel principle': '... if this plan or this undertaking is of human origin, it will fail ...' (Acts 5:34–39).

❧ *Tuesday 12 July*

Enoch, the father of Methuselah, certainly went to heaven in style. One moment he was hunting, shooting and fishing (or whatever they did in those far-off days); and then –

whoosh! – he was caught up to the celestial realms before you could say, 'Josh Robinson!' I don't suppose there was much weeping and gnashing amongst those wild animals and fish with their own teeth.

Enoch did not die, according to Scripture, but was 'translated' – like the great prophet Elijah, who was carried up by a whirlwind without tasting death. Genesis 5:24 says, rather succinctly: 'Enoch walked with God; then he was no more, because God took him.' I trust nothing similar happens to the great-grandson of Enoch Harrison and Son Ltd, of Cononley, near Keighley – certainly not before they finish building our new parish hall.

Genesis 1 declares that after the Creation: 'God saw everything that he had made, and indeed, it was very good' (verse 31). Well, I must record that John Harrison and his team have done a terrific job here, too, as their work nears completion. Unknown to them, there has been a 'spy' in their midst – David, begotten of Jack Hope, of George Hope (my grandfather) and Sons, Builders, of Wakefield. As a teenager I picked up quite a bit about building from my Dad and his labourers. During school holidays I often helped with basic tasks like mixing concrete. Today at St Margaret's we are lucky to have had John as foreman; like my Dad, he has high standards. His team have been particularly cheerful and co-operative. Not only has their work been excellent, but they have respected the church area, clearing up as they go along.

The work is due to be completed at the end of August, and the hall will be available from early September; hopefully, bookings from outside organisations will reduce the shortfall of around £100,000. The hall is to be opened officially by Fr Richard and Muriel on Saturday 15 October. After that, all that will remain for us is, like Enoch, to walk with God – which might not be as easy!

❧ *Wednesday 13 July*

To Hull, to receive an honorary Doctor of Divinity degree from Hull University. I wrote a paper for the Theological Society based on research for my D Phil on the development of early liturgy in the Western Church. I have also been fairly active in the Hull area, so I suppose the university must regard me as one of their own.

The Professor of Theology, Lester Grabbe, reads the citation, and the degree is conferred by the chancellor of the university, Lord Armstrong of Ilminster. At the end of the proceedings I say a few words, crack a few jokes, remember to take away my scroll and head for lunch. This is my second honorary Doctor of Divinity degree (the first being from Nottingham University, where I took my BA); they're a bit of fun, but not to be taken *too* seriously. The author of Ecclesiastes, that short cynical book just after Proverbs, would call today's cult of 'celebrity' status 'vanity and a chasing after wind' (Ecclesiastes 2:26). God's real stars are those who are unaware of themselves, such as those who care long-term for sick relatives, bear affliction patiently or show forgiveness in difficult circumstances. The greatest fulfilment I receive today is in anointing our treasurer Barbara France, due for a complicated ankle operation on Friday. Barbara is amazing – a faithful and absolutely reliable Christian. If the Church is, as St Paul wrote, the body of Christ, Barbara could well be described as an ankle of St Margaret's.

❧ *Friday 15 July*

The final meeting of Playtime before the summer holidays coincides with St Swithin's Day, so if it rains today Incy may need a thorough drying-out when battle recommences in September.

After the brakes have been applied to the wheels on the bus and the last green bottle has been stowed safely away, I join in a happy 'end-of-term' lunch: cold chicken, pork pies, that kind of thing. Fortunately, no one is sick and there are no tantrums – though of course you wouldn't expect that of the adult helpers, now that the toddlers have all toddled off – and peace rules for the moment.

It's the big day for Barbara, who is awake before 7 am and in the operating theatre at the Leeds BUPA Hospital by 8.30 am for her ankle operation. The nurses who welcomed her last night described her as 'remarkably calm'. By lunchtime she is out of theatre, the operation apparently having been successful. I'm not surprised – Barbara has had the best spiritual attention that money can't buy: she's on our prayer list and has our own kind of BUPA (Being Under the Protection of Angels)!

✿ Saturday 16 July

This morning I visit Barbara, who is sitting up in bed and amazingly together but still heavily doped. It must be quite pleasant not to have to think of domestic duties and church responsibilities, such as raising funds for the new hall and the parish share. All Barbara wants at present is to have her hair done. It looks fine to me!

✿ Sunday 17 July

Before today's main service Mrs Jean Driver is busy weeding the path leading to our memorial area where her late husband Jim's ashes are interred. Fortunately, she didn't put off the task until afterwards – today's Gospel is about slaves who were ordered to leave weeds where they were in a field to avoid the risk of wheat being pulled up with them. Jesus' parable of the wheat and weeds (Matthew 13:24–43) is highly appropriate, following the London bombings on what will always be known as '7/7'. It explains that good and evil co-exist now but in the end evil will be consumed by the fire of God's goodness.

Instead of preaching on the parable, Fr Alan Millar talks about Harry, a colleague in the steel sales department of Dorman Long, Middlesbrough, before Alan was ordained. Harry had a loud voice, and once, after he rang someone in Birmingham, a typist said to him: 'Why didn't you open the window? That way you wouldn't have had to use the phone!'

We often scream and shout at God, says Alan, when what we need most is to listen to the still, small voice ready to guide us – silence really is golden. Before he was ordained, Alan attended a retreat led by Archbishop Michael Ramsey. The Prelate had a great sense of humour, but could be serious – even stern – when necessary. Ordinands arriving at Bishopthorpe were told: 'This is a retreat, in which we keep silence. If you don't want to do so, go home – I won't ordain you.'

Alan says we are unlikely to hear the divine voice directly, but if we wait on God in silence, thoughts and ideas will often come into our minds, which will be the Lord addressing us. Everyone's thoughts wander during prayer, but we can still the mind by repeating a short phrase such as 'Lord Jesus Christ, Son of the Living God, have mercy on me' or 'Be still, and know that I am God.'

After the service, there's a birthday cake from Arthur Marshall, who was 80 last week. On Wednesday – St Margaret's Day – he is to provide the wine at a party after the evening Eucharist. It should be good – Arthur is a former wine merchant.

❧ *Wednesday 20 July*

> 'Rouse yourself! Why do you sleep, O Lord? Awake, do
> not cast us off for ever!' (Psalm 44:23)

A familiar cry down the centuries, these particular words
were in fact written several centuries before Jesus was born.
But international terrorism is making the question scream in
many people's minds today. If there *is* a God, why doesn't he
do something about it?

As I see it, there have been four options open to the Lord
in response to human wickedness:

1. *Do nothing* – and wait for humans (all of them!) to reject
   the vicious cycle of violence and seemingly endless
   retaliation. He could be waiting until Doomsday.
2. *Destroy humanity and start again.* This is God's choice in the
   story of Noah (Genesis 6—9), which may be a lesson
   showing what God could have done but didn't, rather
   than what we would call history. If it is history, the Creator
   has ruled out the possibility of another wipe-out (Genesis
   9:14–17).
3. *Remove the 'dark side' in human nature.* Unfortunately, this
   would destroy human freedom to choose between good
   and evil, turning us effectively into robots.
4. *Overcome evil with good.* The most radical solution of all,
   since this would involve God in becoming human himself
   and not retaliating when he was being tortured and killed
   by his enemies. Show divine love is stronger than human
   malice, hate and self-will by being 'finished off' but
   'bouncing back' again – alive for evermore. Change the
   world from within by filling ordinary men and women
   with love for God and others.

The last option was the one which led to Christ's crucifixion – and the founding of the Church. Today we remember one of the first Christian martyrs, our patron St Margaret of Antioch, whose faith in 'Christ crucified' led her to the block. She is depicted in Graeme Willson's painting as offering pearls (the meaning of her name) to the infant Jesus. Beneath the Madonna and Child is a dragon carved on a rock. In Revelation, Satan appears before the woman in the form of a dragon and seeks to devour her child (Revelation 12:1–6). Despite the bizarre imagery in the Bible's closing book, the whole thrust of Revelation is the eventual triumph of God and his purposes over all that is evil in the world.

St Margaret was the daughter of a third- or fourth-century pagan priest in Pisidian Antioch who was disowned by her father after converting to Christianity. A story grew up that in prison she was swallowed by a dragon but was ejected when the cross she carried irritated its innards. Maybe what was originally a symbolic story was later, in a less sceptical age, interpreted literally. At any event, it is easy to see how St Margaret became the patron saint of pregnancy, labour and childbirth. Couples having trouble in conceiving a child might benefit from having a word with Margaret after a relaxing break in the quiet of Ilkley. She seems to have been hard at prayer since our one-hundred-and-twenty-fifth anniversary in 2004. After all, we *have* had a lot of baptisms recently!

❧ *Thursday 21 July*

Before the St Margaret's Day celebrations yesterday I represented Bishop David James at the Bradford University Degree Ceremony, having another chat with the retiring chancellor, Baroness Betty Lockwood. The majority – perhaps 80 per cent – of those receiving degrees were Asian. Everyone was relaxed and enjoying themselves, not least D. Hope (BA Hons,

Theology, Nottingham, 1962) for whom it was like a trip to the dentist – all I had to do was sit. Very restful, but I took care not to open my mouth in the chair. It wouldn't have done to be discovered asleep in public.

Today I am near Clumber Park in Nottinghamshire to preside at a family thanksgiving for Lord Hanson and his wife, Geraldine, who predeceased him. There were separate memorial services, but the family want to say goodbye to them both at the grave on the family's estate, and I am happy to offer my love and support.

Afterwards an Ascot-style buffet is laid on in two grand tents, but since I am driving I decline the kind offers of champagne with a heavy heart. Can you imagine the furore if I were to fail a breath-test? The newspaper sub-editors may already have headlines waiting for me 'just in case':

> Take a little wine for your stomach's sake (St Paul)
> (but be sure to have less than 80 mg of alcohol per 100 ml of blood)

and

HOPE'S BINGE ETERNAL

I am reminded of a parishioner – a 3–4 units a week man – who was involved in a minor collision when leaving Tesco in Ilkley a few years ago on the run-up to Holy Week. No one was hurt, and little damage was caused, but the other driver insisted on calling the police and demanded that our man be breathalysed. When he had given the usual personal details, he was asked when he last drank alcohol. After a moment's reflection, he replied: 'I am a Christian currently observing Lent. It must have been on Ash Wednesday – let me see now, 22 days ago.' The interrogating officer went through the motions of administering a breath-test, but the result was a foregone conclusion. When the police car departed, it was with a fairly annoyed cop at the wheel.

❧ Friday 22 July

It's 7.15 am, and six early birds are with me for the earliest morning Mass of the week on St Mary Magdalene's Day.

It's a pity the Church does not grant this great saint a prime-time slot on a Sunday in view of her contribution to the development of Christianity. From the slightly differing accounts of the first Easter Sunday, it is clear she was among the first witnesses of the Resurrection – perhaps the first.

The clearest insight into her character can be seen in Luke 8:1–3, which refers to her as 'Mary, called Magdalene, from whom seven demons had gone out'. We do not know whether she had been mentally ill or 'possessed'. Nor can we be sure either way whether she was the prostitute who washed Jesus' feet with her tears (Luke 7:36–50). As to any suggestions that she had a sexual relationship with Jesus, I merely point out that Hugh Montefiore, later Bishop of Birmingham, caused a furore in 1967 by claiming that Jesus might have been 'homosexual in nature' (he did not state or even imply that the Lord was a practising homosexual). Rather strangely to this generation, personality traits and behaviour were of absolutely no interest to Luke, who simply wanted to show that Jesus freed Mary from whatever had been eating her up inside, and could make the readers of his gospel whole. St Paul provided the perfect commentary on Mary Magdalene's significance when he wrote: '… if anyone is in Christ, there is a new creation: everything old has passed away; see, everything has become new!' (2 Corinthians 5:17).

❧ *Sunday 24 July*

> So Moses cried out to the LORD, 'What shall I do with
> this people? They are almost ready to stone me.'
>
> (Exodus 17:4)

There's been murmuring among a section of my flock. It's nothing like the hassle which Moses received from the Children of Israel before they melted down their golden earrings and plates to make a golden calf (Exodus 32). The Children of Ilkley wouldn't do that, of course; can you imagine Yorkshire folk giving away spare precious metal – especially to the Church?

By contrast, the local grumbling has been in typically polite Ilkley fashion – more on the lines of, 'Sorry to trouble you, Fr David. I trust you won't mind my mentioning this, but some of us have been wondering if the Family Service members might be persuaded to mix perhaps a little more with the main congregation, instead of dashing off to the seaside straight afterwards with their children or going to the wife's parents' house for Sunday lunch? We feel this could help to create more of a sense of community.'

So instead of the two normal services, this morning we have a single, united act of worship at 10 am. I am presiding in my bishop's golden hat (it's not 24-carat gold – if it had been, we might have melted it down to pay off the loan on the parish hall). I'm also in red vestments in honour of St Margaret. Those in the front row must be wishing they'd brought their sunglasses, if not their deckchairs and ice creams!

For a few minutes I speak about joy, as felt by Mother Teresa of Calcutta, who never forgot while working among the world's poorest people that Christ's Resurrection was their ultimate hope. How can Christians not be joyful? No matter how dark and troubled the world is, Christ has triumphed over the forces of evil and has promised to be with us always!

The centre of attention this morning, though, is not me but Mathilda Conversy (12¾) from Le Mans, who is leading the prayers. She is the granddaughter of John and Mary Rainforth, and is spending a few weeks with them, together with her brother Paul (17). Mathilda is a gifted artist, and has recently had a lesson from Graeme Willson. At her own special request, I christened her last Sunday. 'I didn't want to be baptised in France,' Mathilda says. 'They're too serious over there, and it's *fun* at St Margaret's!'

Pass around *le mot, s'il te plâit*?

We have to concentrate during the prayers, because Mathilda has found a mini-sermon in English which she translated into French – with a little help from *grandpère*. She reads both versions out, starting with the French:

> *Un sourire ne coûte rien, et apporte beaucoup. Il enrichit celui qui le reçoit, sans appauvrir celui qui le donne. Il ne dure qu'un instant, mais son souvenir est parfois immortel. Et pourtant il ne peut ni s'acheter, ni se prêter, ni se voler car il n'a de valeur qu'à partir du moment où il se donne. Et si on vous refuse le sourire que vous méritez, soyer généreux, donnez-lui le vôtre – pour l'amour de Dieu.*

(A smile doesn't cost anything, but it helps a lot. It makes the one who receives it rich, without making the one who gives it poor. It lasts only a second, but its memory sometimes lives forever. It cannot be bought, or lent or stolen, because it only has any value from the moment it is given. And if someone refuses the smile you deserve, be generous and give yours to them – for the love of God.)

Hopefully, Mathilda will be back at St Margaret's next summer, and for many years to come. She is the Church of the future – bright, polite and cheerful. If Mathilda had been around during the mid-1950s, Françoise Sagan might have written a follow-up to her novel *Bonjour Tristesse* – *Bonjour Joie*!

Viens nous revoir, Mathilda – à toute à l'heure!

♣ *Wednesday 27 July*

It's always encouraging to hear of children raising money for charity in spontaneous acts of kindness. I was moved to read in the *Ilkley Gazette* two weeks ago about Rachael Conlon (five) and her brother Aidan (six) whose self-initiated toy sale at home fetched £122 for Orbis International, an eye charity helping children in the Third World. The sum was matched by their mum, and as a result 12 children overseas can expect to have their sight saved.

I have been involved with Yorkshire Eye Research for several years, and today agreed to help an appeal to the county's artists to donate a painting for sale towards the charity. Research into eye disease is currently not sexy, but the work is crucial – especially in Africa – so I am pleased to be able to lend a hand.

♣ *Thursday 28 July*

A most mysterious entry has just been spotted in the church's visitors book. It's dated 24 July, and reads: 'David Hope, Notre Dame Cathedral, Ho Chi Minh City, Vietnam'. Some parishioners think it's a hoax, but I'm not so sure – the handwriting is neat, apparently by someone educated. There's only one way to find out, by searching for Mr Hope on the internet and sending an e-mail.

🌰 *Sunday 31 July*

I have a most enjoyable duty to perform at the main service today – blessing two rings to be exchanged on 9 September at a wedding in Italy.

The marriage might not have been taking place at Siena's Palazzo Publico [Town Hall] if Naomi Millar had not given what she calls 'a subtle nudge' to her long-standing friend Andy Peverill.

They were walking past a jeweller's in this beautiful old town in Tuscany last June, when suddenly Naomi stopped. 'You see that?' she asked, indicating an engagement ring with three diamonds set in white gold. 'How would you like to buy me one as an engagement present when you finally get round to marrying me?' Andy could only reply: 'I was going to ask you on Friday, the last day of our holiday.' If this is Naomi's idea of subtlety, I wonder how she calls a spade a spade?

The couple met after Andy, a senior construction engineer, started to ring Naomi for information; he couldn't expect the technical sales manager with a ventilation engineering company to be shy and retiring. Naomi's parents, Fr Alan and Jean Millar, celebrated their golden wedding anniversary last July; Naomi and Andy's wedding rings are to be of pure white gold.

Watching today's short ceremony is a youth group from South-West Virginia, led by Joe and Laura Harden. Exchanges between that Diocese and Bradford have taken place for more than 30 years. The Episcopalian visitors, from Roanoke, a former railroad town of around 200,000 people, are on a three-week whistle-stop tour of Bradford Diocese due to end on 10 August.

Like many other visitors before him, Joe finds St Margaret's a 'very spiritual' building and the music 'awe-inspiring'. He says: 'It was a wonderful service, in which I could sense God's presence the whole time. Most of our churches don't have your candles, "bells and smells" – you seem more catholic than some of the Roman Catholic churches back home!'

During the afternoon, a party of visitors from another great diocese – Wakefield – arrive for tea and cakes in time for Evensong. We make sure all those High Church candles are out before they leave – we don't want a repeat of the blaze which broke out in 2003 when Wakefield came to Ilkley!

August

✿ Monday 1 August

It's Yorkshire Day and, all over the three ancient Ridings and
the City of York, Yorkshire men and women will be having
slap-up celebratory lunches, trusting their non-Yorkshire
friends will pay. Many will have in mind – and some, perhaps,
will recite – the Tyke's Motto:

> See all, hear all
> say nowt.
> Eat all, sup all
> pay nowt.
> And if ivver tha does
> owt fer nowt,
> Allus do it fer
> thysen.

Not for nothing has the Yorkshireman been dubbed 'a
Scotsman without the generosity'.

Of course, the above are examples of the greatest Yorkshire
characteristic – the ability to laugh at ourselves. But there is a
grain of truth behind the motto. One of the 'threats' to the
growth of St Margaret's identified at our parish mission day in
June was 'Yorkshire tightness with cash'. Yorkshire folk take
an interest in others and are resilient, but they can also be
rather brittle. As Ilkley's town crier, Chris Richards, puts it:
'We call a spade a bloody shovel.'

Chris (62), from Bingley, is in his blue and gold regalia

today, ready to make the Yorkshire Declaration, produced by
the newly-formed Yorkshire Ridings Society in 1975 following local government reform in 1974. The only consolation
for true Yorkshiremen and women about, in particular, the
advent of 'Humberside' in what had been the East Riding for
considerably more than 1,000 years is that the changes took
effect on April Fools' Day (fortunately, Humberside has since
been consigned to the scrap-heap of history). The first of
August, by contrast, has a special association in Yorkshire. On
that day in 1759 soldiers from England's largest county picked
white roses near the battlefields of Minden in Germany as a
tribute to friends killed in action.

Chris's powerful voice was developed as a teacher in Brat-
ford (as they call it locally) and is maintained by shouting at
his collie, Mr Ben. In 2001 Chris stood out among the other
candidates interviewed for the position of Ilkley town crier
(about four 'cries' a year; honorarium, £250) by blasting out
a ditty he had composed for the occasion:

> Oyez! Oyez! Oyez!
> I am here for an interview
> to see if I am suitable
> to be a crier in this fair town
> and wear a ceremonial gown.
> God save the Queen!

Today's task is more demanding, but Chris is not daunted –
he reckons that on a fine day he could stand beside the Cow
and Calf Rocks on Ilkley Moor and be heard a mile away.
After ringing his crier's bell, Chris simply lets rip:

> Oyez! Oyez! Oyez!
> I, Chris Richards,
> being a resident in the West Riding of Yorkshire,

> declare that Yorkshire is three Ridings
> and the City of York
> with these boundaries of 1126 years standing;
> that the address of all places in these Ridings is
>   Yorkshire;
> that any person or corporate body
> which deliberately ignores or denies the
>   aforementioned
> shall forfeit all claim to Yorkshire status.
> These declarations made this Yorkshire Day.
> Yorkshire for ever!
> God save the Queen!

Afterwards, 'On Ilkla Moor Baht 'At' (the Yorkshire Anthem) is sung and there's a mild stampede towards those local shops on the Yorkshire Food Trail giving away free samples.

I thoroughly approve of Yorkshire Day, as I would of similar days in other parts of Britain with local pride; in a fast-changing world we all need roots and a sense of continuity with the past. All the same, I have to confess I am missing today's excitement in Ilkley, although like St Luke I have checked everything carefully (Luke 1:3) and am sure I've an 'OK source'. It's exactly a year since my appointment as parish priest of St Margaret's was announced, and it's my day off. So I'm treating myself to a long walk – in 'God's own country', of course!

❧ *Thursday 4 August*

A special award for a remarkable lady. Local MP Ann Cryer is to become an honorary lay canon of Bradford Cathedral in recognition of her service on the cathedral council during the past five years and her work with vulnerable – especially young Asian – women. She is to be installed on 18 September.

Ann says:

> I feel it is a special connection with my late husband
> John, who had been a clergyman for 42 years when he
> died in November. It draws together so many impor-
> tant threads in my life – John, my work for the
> Cathedral, for women, and being an MP.

The Church is the whole community of Christians, both
clergy and laity in a particular place, and lay participation
should be encouraged at every level. Their involvement in
finance and management is especially to be encouraged, since
few in the clergy are skilled in these areas. Ann is well respected locally and has a good knowledge of inter-faith issues;
I'm sure she'll make a considerable contribution to the work
of the cathedral.

My highlight today is a visit to the Skipton Building
Society headquarters for a meeting of the Charitable Trust.
We award several useful grants to organisations such as the
Swaledale Mountain Rescue Team, Contact the Elderly
Yorkshire, the Leeds-based Caring for Life, and the Friends of
Menston School, near Ilkley.

The headquarters building is smart, with a good atmosphere for working. It's largely open-plan, light and airy. As
you would expect, the boardroom where we meet is plush,
with a tasteful décor, huge mahogany table and sleep-
inducing leather armchairs. Something is missing, however –
tea-making facilities. We have to ring up to get someone to
fetch us a cuppa.

❧ Sunday 7 August

God has been called 'the God of surprises' and he certainly
has one lined up today for Polish chemical engineer Piotr
Kcapczynski.

A week ago Piotr arrived in England to begin a summer job selling ice cream to finance his studies at home in human resources management. Ilkley is filled with trippers on Sundays, and is especially busy today during our summer festival. Piotr is ready for the ice cream Grand Prix – he's next to the bandstand in Pole position.

Shortly before noon a collection of Christians arrive for a *Songs of Praise* service run by Churches Together in Ilkley. It's a lovely hot day, but you can't worship and consume ice cream simultaneously so for the next half-hour Piotr is marooned (like the Ancient Mariner) and powerless:

> Lots of lovely ice cream here, to counteract the heat;
> Christians, Christians everywhere – but none of them
>   will eat!

The mood across Britain is sombre, with the country stunned by the death yesterday of former Foreign Secretary Robin Cook, who collapsed while climbing Ben Stack (2,370 ft) in Sutherland. He was only 59, and his loss is a reminder to all of our human frailty, possible illness and certain death.

Yet, by coincidence, today we celebrate the Feast of the Transfiguration – an oasis in a dry time in the Christian calendar – which reminds us of how Peter, James and John were granted a vision on another mountain (perhaps Mount Hermon) of Jesus in clothes which suddenly became dazzlingly white. They were brighter even than the raspberry-pink hat with lime-green trim and band which Philippa Higgins is wearing at St Margaret's this morning.

Fr Bernard calls the Transfiguration a 'picture of perfection', permitted by God to strengthen Jesus for his coming ordeal and to give the disciples courage to walk with him on the road to Calvary. Glimpses of glory are given today through Christ's Real Presence in the eucharistic mysteries and through waiting on God in Bible-reading and prayer. 'If we keep the vision of God's beauty and splendour before us, we can endure whatever lies before us,' Fr Bernard says.

Among the hymns at the bandstand is 'Our God is a Great Big God' ('higher than a skyscraper ... wider than the universe'). I am continually astonished that such a vast person cares for each of us. Perhaps God's main intention for me today is to be kind to the Polish ice cream vendor without baffling him with cornet jokes. 'You look rather forlorn,' I shout across to him before giving the blessing. 'I hope people will buy a few ices from you afterwards – I trust they're not too expensive?' Some people take up my suggestion, but I go straight home for lunch – 'Seldom on a Sundae' is my motto.

❧ Tuesday 9 August

> But of others there is no memory; they have perished as though they had never existed, they have become as though they had never been born ...
>
> (Ecclesiasticus 44:9)

A realistic but rather depressing analysis of human life, since apart from a few individuals like novelists and artists, the only legacy that most people leave behind is their children.

But in Queen's Road, Ilkley, the workforce of Enoch Harrison and Son Limited have laid down a remarkable legacy which should last for centuries: our new parish hall. Their work speaks for itself, and will continue to do so, but here is my tribute with this roll of honour:

Builders: John Harrison, Stan Sharpe, Steven Holmes, Richard Dyminski, Steven Gott and Peter Stirling
Plasterers: Colin Rushton, John Ackroyd and Chris Green

Steel Fabrication: James Bentley

Plumber: Adrian Roberts

Joiners: Ian McParland, Tim Mawson, Andrew Fountain, Matthew Richardson, David Cooke and James Turner Pratt

Roofers: Michael Devaney, Deryck Facey and Steven Jones

Electricians: Jim Buttery, Ian Lyle and James Mole

Tradesmen all – like Jesus was.

And what has been the point of all their labour? To provide a comfortable building where St Margaret's members can chat over coffee on Sunday? Only incidentally – the real purpose is connected with a 'foundation-shaking' event in the twelfth century, when Francis Bernardone heard a voice at the neglected chapel of St Damian's below Assisi: 'Go, Francis, and repair my house, which as you see is falling into ruin.'

What a sorry, dilapidated state the house that is the Church of England must seem to many young people to be in today: out of touch and irrelevant, but ever striving to be 'meaningful'. I'm reminded of the two sisters Martha and Mary, whom Jesus visited in Bethany (Luke 10:38–42). Martha was rushing around trying to make the perfect meal for Jesus, but Mary forgot everything else, sat down and listened to him. When Martha complained about this, Jesus replied that only a few things were needed – perhaps only one. He meant that if she put listening to God first, everything else would fall into place. Surely it's time for Anglicans to stop wearing themselves out in endless political and semi-political activity. These things have their place sometimes – but second place. We need to stop examining our navels, resume the business of waiting on God in prayer, Word and Sacrament, and, strengthened by God's holy food, take his love on to the local bus or train, into the office and into our local superstore.

Hence the sign currently outside the building:

ST MARGARET'S CHURCH
NEW PARISH HALL
EXPANDING OUR WORK
TO SERVE THE COMMUNITY

At our parish mission day in June, I suggested we should aim to double the congregation over the next five years, after which I must join the ranks of the retired clergy (currently around 200 adults and children attend the three Sunday morning services). This is not impossible if every member aims to introduce one new person to St Margaret's. It is not about survival (though the house will eventually collapse if it is not rebuilt); it's about doing God's will by taking his healing grace out into a world where so many people are unhappy and afraid. Richard Hoyal planted, and I am watering; God will give the growth at St Margaret's (and elsewhere) if Christ's followers follow the example of Mary, rather than Martha.

❧ *Thursday 11 August*

What has Bradford in common with its linked diocese in Africa, the Sudan? The impartial observer, unaware of the whole picture in each case, might reply simply 'riots'.

Ten days ago at least 24 people died as rioting swept Khartoum following news that the vice-president, John Garang, had been killed in a helicopter crash near the Ugandan border. Some southern Sudanese suspected foul play behind the death of Mr Garang, a key figure in a tenuous peace deal between the predominantly Arab Muslim government and the Christian south.

From the comfort of respectable Ilkley it's easy to be judgemental about the troubles in the Sudan, or many parts of the world. But four years ago 326 police officers were injured in rioting at Bradford (only 11 miles away) which caused damage costing around £7.5 million. Who knows when and where, in this uncertain life, 'civilisation' will collapse into chaos?

Today I meet Jo Udal, a priest familiar with both Bradford Diocese and the Sudan, where she works with the Church Missionary Society in Khartoum. Jo lets a house in Limehouse, and by chance Judith Kilvington, daughter of our PCC Secretary, is one of her tenants. Jo has a special connection with All Saints', Ilkley, but wanted to meet me since she was an ordinand in London when I was bishop there.

Jo is delighted to see a prayer request I have received by e-mail from the Bishop of Khartoum, and I shall appreciate receiving updates once she is back in the Sudan. I marvel sometimes at the commitment of those – of many religions and none – who run risks daily to make life more bearable for others in the world's trouble-spots. I shall indeed try to pray for Jo once she is 'back home'.

✤ *Friday 12 August*

Ilkley's main street, The Grove, becomes pedestrian-only and is packed today for the annual continental street market, now in its third year. The event is obviously good for the town, with more than 25,000 visitors expected between now and Sunday night. I'm impressed by the variety of items available – both food and non-food – but wonder about some of the cheeses. In brie-f, they're somewhat expensive so I shall stick to Booths or Tesco.

✤ *Sunday 14 August*

Today we celebrate the Assumption of the Virgin Mary, called by the early Church *Theotokos* (Gk, 'God-bearer', or 'Mother of God').

The title was assigned to Jesus' mother at the Third
Ecumenical Council at Ephesus in 431. Nestorius, Patriarch
of Constantinople, wanted her to be called *Christotokos*
('Christ-bearer'), to restrict her status to that of the mother of
Christ's humanity. This would, unfortunately, have divided
Jesus into two persons. We believe, however, that she bore the
Second Person of the Holy (and itself undivided) Trinity. The
child conceived was both human and divine – but not in a
'Jekyll and Hyde' kind of way.

Difficult, of course – but how can you pin down precisely
what is essentially a great mystery? Calling Mary 'Mother of
God' was never meant to imply she 'pre-dated' God – that
would make her God. Instead, the Church acknowledges the
mystery of God *Incarnate* ('in flesh') in words from an ancient
hymn:

> He whom the entire universe could not contain
> was contained within your womb, O *Theotokos*.

Mary is honoured for her total openness to God's will, but not
worshipped in any way – the Archangel Gabriel's address to
her at the Annunciation (Luke 1:26–38), often translated as
'hail', is more accurately rendered 'greetings'.

Mary's final destiny is a sign of hope for ours. It can perhaps be summed up simply in a Salvation Army phrase –
'gone to glory'. You can add 'body and soul', provided you
realise there was a unity about Mary: she was a whole person,
'body-mind-spirit' rather than a soul in a body. The same
holds true with us – the view that 'John Brown's body lies a-
mouldering in the grave, but his soul goes marching on' may
be comforting to some, but the assumptions behind it are
Greek, not Judaeo-Christian.

In the Apostles' Creed, one of the Church's earliest credal
formularies, we declare 'I believe ... in the resurrection of the

body, and the life everlasting'. Surely no one has ever explained the implications of this statement better than St Paul. In 1 Corinthians 15 he does not shy away from talking about the body, but contrasts the 'natural body' with the 'spiritual body' (1 Corinthians 15:44). Regarding the resurrection of the dead he does not ask, 'With what kind of soul or spirit are the dead raised?' Rather, his question is, 'How are the dead raised? With what kind of *body* do they come?' And to help us begin to answer such questions, he uses the analogy of a seed. It is put in the ground and dies, but in due time rises again in a form very different from that which was originally sown. As one commentator puts it:

> Paul is showing that at one and the same time there can be dissolution, difference and yet continuity. So our earthly bodies will dissolve; they will rise again in very different form; but it is the same person who rises. Dissolved by death, changed by resurrection, it is still we who exist.

✣ *Monday 15 – Friday 19 August*

It's not just at St Margaret's where the Church is full of enthusiasm – and joy – in Ilkley. This week the annual children's holiday club run by the ecumenical Churches Together in Ilkley takes place at the Baptist Church. The helpers have given up a lot of time and put in a considerable amount of energy to make the week what it becomes – a great success. I take my hat off to them, especially as it's decorated with a skull-and-crossbones, which might possibly cause questions to be asked in the Town Hall, and certainly would in the House of Lords, if the news got out.

I wonder what St Paul would make of my hat? The apostle had strong views on headgear, which would go down like a lead balloon in this politically correct age. Just imagine the outcry there'd be if someone proclaimed in public these days what is available for all to read in 1 Corinthians 11:

> Any man who prays or prophesies with something on his head disgraces his head, but any woman who prays or prophesies with her head unveiled disgraces her head ... if a woman will not veil herself, then she should cut off her hair ... a man ought not to have his head veiled, since he is the image and reflection of God; but woman is the reflection of man ... Neither was man created for the sake of woman, but woman for the sake of man.

The apostle could not complain about Philippa Higgins, wife of Canon Godfrey Higgins, former Vicar of Pontefract. This youthful grandmother has plenty of hats – 31, if you count one for swimming and two for repelling mosquitoes. But this week the total has been reduced temporarily, since Godfrey has pillaged her hat cupboard for suitable pirate headgear in which to attend the holiday club. 'Hatwoman' is cheerful and easy-going, and evidently doesn't mind. Philippa has clear, blue eyes, and the smile and manner of a 35-year-old. A school report once described her as 'boisterous but well intentioned' – presumably desirable qualities in helpers at a holiday club with pirates as the theme.

The nine other adult helpers at Ilkley Baptist Church are divided over whether Godfrey looks more dashing in his wife's orange or blue bandanna, or the fetching blue number decorated with gentians. Godfrey, the pianist, is sporting an eyepatch but was too Yorkshire to fork out £2.49 for a pirate cutlass (soft rubber, in the interests of health and safety) at Ilkley's Whoopee Party Shop.

The hall is decorated with palm trees, fishes, treasure maps,

a ship's bell and pirate flag when about 60 children rush in on
Monday morning. They are divided into four crews: Golden
Galleons (yellow), Silver Schooners (white), Crystal Clippers
(blue) and Ruby Rafts (red). Oh to be young – even if it
means thinking wild shepherds watched their flocks by night
or wondering why the green hill far away was without a city
wall. How many of those present, I wonder, think Jesus
'suffered under Pontius Pirate'? Maybe some even imagine he
was forced to walk the plank instead of being nailed to two ...

It's a brilliant idea to have a pirate adventure running
alongside the story of the early life, conversion and travels of
St Paul. Songs, craft and games like Man the Lifeboats gradu-
ally introduce the idea that pirate treasure does not last, but
Jesus' treasure is for ever, the theme of 'The Landlubbers
Song' by Ruth Wills of Scripture Union:

> We're pirates from the open sea, landed on the shore,
> Ah-oooh! Ah-oooh!
> Trying to reclaim the treasure that's in store,
> Ah-oooh! Ah-oooh!
> And we're keeping going, on towards the prize,
> and we're keeping going, never take our eyes
> off the treasure, ah-oooh! The treasure, ah-oooh! ...

The more thoughtful youngsters will have twigged that Jesus
was only *buried* treasure until that first Easter morning ...

Star of the show is a flesh-and-blood Captain – not Cap'n
Birdseye, but Cap'n John Smith, a youth worker at All Saints',
who plays St Paul; the children particularly enjoy visiting him
in 'jail' – a room at the Baptist Church with conveniently
leaded windows. Taking dictation from him with a feather
quill is 'Timothy' (Ben Labbett, from Sacred Heart Church),
while keeping guard outside in Roman soldier's uniform is
Robbie Kay, from All Saints'.

On Thursday there's a rehearsal for the final day's activities, which include a service of celebration. Watching it (without an eye-patch!), I'm confident that parents, grandparents and carers will be able to judge for themselves how much fun the young have had – and so it proves next day.

A special word for Christine Butler, a St Margaret's member who has run the under-fives Discoverers group at All Saints' for 17 years! You might think she'd get bored, but there's a freshness and vitality about her teaching which I find remarkable. Christine has a 1995 1.4CL Polo with 42,000 miles on the clock, but next month is buying a new, one-litre Peugeot 107. The registration number will include '55', and her children are hugely amused, as that will be her age on 25 September.

Sometimes you have to forgive your family as well as your enemies!

❧ Friday 19 August

The second day of a two-day break as one of the judges in the Favourite Market Town 2005 competition organised by *Country Life* magazine and the property company Strutt and Parker. My fellow judges include Penelope Keith, the actress; Noel Edmonds, the broadcaster; Ben Fogle, presenter of the BBC's *Countryfile;* and John Selwyn Gummer MP, the former Conservative Agriculture Secretary.

I have travelled to Beverley (East Riding of Yorkshire), Hexham (Northumberland) and Barnard Castle (County Durham), searching for the ideal market town, based on a blend of charm, accessibility and community spirit. These three towns are very different, but all worth a visit. I don't feel guilty about being away from St Margaret's, as going further afield occasionally will lessen the danger of my becoming too parochial. I shall have to do battle on behalf of my selection against the other judges' choices in October at a lunch at the Ritz in London.

✿ *Thursday 25 August*

It's a pleasant surprise today when Bill Davidson, a contemporary of mine at Nottingham University, calls to see me while visiting friends in Ilkley, where he grew up. He has become more rotund through good living but apparently hasn't changed otherwise – he's as lively as ever.

Bill read Law at Nottingham, where I took Theology, and in our spare time we had some splendid evenings at gatherings of the Philoenic Society (*'philein'*, 'to love'; *'oinos'*, 'wine' [Greek]), a dining club. Besides the formal dinners, we often went to Yates Wine Lodge to drink schooners of cheap sherry. It wasn't binge-drinking – I had a normal university experience.

✿ *Saturday 27 August*

Those who tried to write off Pope Benedict XVI seem set to be proved wrong: he could be a formidable figure, judging by his powerful homily in Cologne at the closing Mass of World Youth Day on Sunday. His interpretation of the mystery at the heart of Christianity – that the Cross was God's answer to human violence – would surely impress St Paul himself. Christopher Howse, writing in the *Daily Telegraph* today, says the Pope's 'modest demeanour and unhectoring style' made a favourable impression, even among the secular press.

In a homily on the Last Supper and the Eucharist, Pope Benedict said:

> By making the bread into his Body and the wine into his Blood, he anticipates his death, he accepts it in his

heart and he transforms it into an action of love. What on the outside is simply brutal violence, from within becomes an act of total self-giving love.

Since the Resurrection transmuted death into love, death could no longer have the last word. The explosion of good conquering evil had begun a series of transformations that would gradually change the world. In the Eucharist God's dynamic entered into Christians, seeking to spread out to others so that his love could become dominant in the world.

A sign of hope indeed – and it *is* better to travel hopefully!

❧ *Sunday 28 August*

Everyone is pleased to see Barbara France back in church, after her ankle operation, with her daughter Kate and granddaughter Rachael (10) from Cumbria. Barbara developed an infection after the operation, and her recovery is taking longer than expected. As you can imagine, she is feeling frustrated by it all.

There is much amusement, however, when Kate reveals over coffee that her mother's maiden name was the same as my former student Father Tickle. Barbara is in the third generation of a line of solicitors, but gathers that her family has no connection with the former London law firm A. J. Tickle and Co. Barbara and Fr Robert don't seem to be related, but will be linked through prayer when I've e-mailed the latter.

At times in everyone's life it's not enough simply to say 'keep your chuckle-muscle exercised'. For everyone who has run dry, St Paul has an appropriate one-liner:

> Rejoice in hope, be patient in suffering, persevere in prayer. (Romans 12:12)

❧ AUTUMN –

The Church Must Be A-Changin'

September

❧ Friday 2 September

A small but very important duty this morning, as I inter Alec Smith's ashes in the churchyard, up a small incline above the church, with a few of Alec's family and friends. The peace that sometimes feels so powerful in St Margaret's extends to the grounds. May Alec rest in peace – and rise in glory.

❧ Saturday 3 September

This morning all the Playtime equipment is shifted from the back of the church and taken through the covered walkway connecting St Margaret's with the new hall, now virtually complete.

A children's favourite comes to mind – the puppet Sooty, tormentor from 1952 of Harry Corbett, his long-suffering stooge. I can almost hear the words 'Izzy Wizzy, let's get busy!' as a working party gets cracking. Everything is put on to trolleys, but while small items can be taken by the lift to a storage room on the first floor, the tables have to be carried upstairs. Marie Anson leads a team in the kitchen, while Fr Alan Brown and I arrange the Playtime gear. Using men's intuition, we move some of the shelves to maximise the available space.

Most of the helpers are seeing the hall for the first time, and are more than impressed. There's plenty of space and light – particularly in the large, main first-floor room – and the workmanship shouts quality. Last week the appeal treasurer, Norman Phillips, received a cheque with a note saying the sender had been 'blown away' by the new building. So, I think, would you be.

❧ Sunday 4 September

It's a lovely summer's day – made even lovelier by the return of the choir to normal duties after their August break.

The afternoon is baking hot (perhaps the hottest day of the year) but instead of going swimming at Ilkley's popular lido or walking on the moor, quite a few church members are indoors at 4.30 pm watching Yorkshire TV. Apparently there's a programme on about a local boy made good who climbs virtually to the top of 'the Organisation' (an underworld gang, I presume) but retires to a quiet town, having tired of all the mud-slinging and in-fighting.

Sounds pretty far-fetched to me – all these power-mad people usually hang on until they are pushed.

❧ Wednesday 7 September

I hesitate to admit it, but for a Lancastrian Brian Whittam has a middling-to-good sense of humour. Introducing a talk which I give to the U3A today about my time as Archbishop, he tells of a bishop who goes to one of his country parishes on a pastoral visit. When the bishop arrives for the service, there are only six or seven people in the congregation. 'Didn't you tell them I was coming?' he asks the vicar, distinctly peeved. 'No, I certainly didn't,' the reply comes, 'but it must have leaked out.'

I can't equal that one, but there was the time I visited the Isle of Man with Noel Jones, Bishop of Sodor and Man, and we called at the cattle market at St John's, near Peel, during an auction. Some of the locals were drinking tea and munching – I presume it was Sodor bread – when I waved to someone

I saw in the distance. 'For goodness sake, stop doing that,' said Noel, 'or you'll go away with a herd of cows to add to your flock.' I hadn't much money with me at the time, and sometimes wonder if my credit would have been good.

❧ *Thursday 8 September*

'Lighten our darkness, we beseech thee, O Lord,' begins the Third Collect of Evening Prayer, for 'Aid against All Perils'. Some church members have been pleading this prayer for about 15 years, as long as the poor lighting issue has been rumbling on. They do have a point, for it can be quite dark in church when the daylight outside is poor. 'Walk in the light,' advises a popular modern hymn; presumably the writer had not been inspired by a visit to St Margaret's.

Today the standing committee of the PCC meet with Mike Overton, our architect, and David Haddon-Reece, the York Advisor on Lighting, to discuss the best way forward. Mike is to present proposals to the PCC, but any plan which emerges will have to be approved by the Diocese. We might just get away with spending a four-figure sum on a modern lighting system. Fortunately, funds are available from legacies connected with the church fabric.

❧ *Sunday 11 September*

The country has gone cricket-crazy, with England only needing a draw in the last Test against Australia at the Oval to regain the Ashes for the first time since 1986.

The weather forecast for the south-east is good from an English pessimist's point-of-view: '… a rather humid day with large amounts of cloud and some sporadic outbreaks of rain, locally heavy and thundery … any sunny intervals will be quite limited'. But there's no point in praying for rain or shine, bad or good light. As a spokesman for the Archbishop of Westminster, Cardinal Cormac Murphy-O'Connor, puts it in the *Sunday Telegraph* this morning: 'God is impartial. He admires the mastery of Shane Warne as much as the brilliance of Freddie Flintoff.'

Christian apologists have sometimes cited cricket when trying to explain how the Holy Trinity can be three *and* one – 'there are three stumps, but also one wicket'. They obviously aren't real sportsmen, because of course, until it is disturbed, a wicket also has two bails!

Despite the clash with the Test, there's a good turnout this morning for another service combining both our 9.30 am and 10.30 am congregations. I should think so, too, considering we are celebrating the dedication of the church building 126 years ago yesterday – nearly three years before the origin of the Ashes. In the address I remind everyone that, to the New Testament writers, the Church was not a building but a community of people – a spiritual temple whose foundation stone is Christ. Jesus walks with us wherever we walk, and a useful 'arrow prayer' – whether at a bus stop or in a traffic-jam – is:

> O most merciful Redeemer, friend and brother,
> may I know you more clearly, love you more dearly,
> and follow you more nearly – day by day.
>
> > (adapted from the Prayer of St Richard,
> > Bishop of Chichester 1245–53)

We move straight from the service into the new hall, where the choir, still robed, lead the singing of 'Christ is made the sure foundation'. After prayers by Fr Alan Brown, I give the blessing and sprinkle holy water throughout the building while everyone sings 'Now thank we all our God'. The service ends with the grace. Within five minutes pensions consultant Philip Tooke is standing on the first fallen Malted Milk; moments later Gerald Hodges is picking up the first missing doll.

As everyone goes home to watch the Test – and possibly even eat – head sidesman Allan Barnes is whizzing around with a vacuum. 'If that biscuit doesn't get swept up now, it'll get into the carpet,' he declares – unlike England. The fourth day's play is ruined by interruptions. How long, I wonder, before our Australian Christian brothers and sisters can sing, 'Walk in the Light' without flinching?

♣ *Monday 12 September*

> [Samson] struck them down hip and thigh with great slaughter ... (Judges 15:8)

And Kevin Pietersen struck [the Aussies] on and off today with a great innings of 158 (seven sixes and 15 fours) to enable England to regain the Ashes.

Australia were finally worn down by a sustained team effort based on a splendid collective spirit. But let us not forget Shane Warne, who passed Dennis Lillee's record of 167 Ashes wickets and was so gracious in defeat. Or Richie Benaud, another all-time great, who turned off his microphone for the last time in England at the end of this, the greatest-ever Test series. Knowledgeable, witty and a true gentleman – he will be missed.

Patriotism is not enough: the desire to win at all costs in sport can only lead to arrogance, envy, malice and bitterness, which will divide, rather than unite, the players and their supporters. For now, let's just be thankful for the Australians – and not be too downhearted if they win next time!

♣ *Tuesday 13 September*

Today a short meditation on the Prayer of Commitment by Ignatius Loyola (1491–1556), founder of the Jesuits:

Teach us, good Lord,
to serve you as you deserve:
to give, and not to count the cost;
to fight, and not to heed the wounds;
to toil, and not to seek for rest ...

I take it the saint is making the general point that service to God should be wholehearted; he does not expect every word to be taken literally. A soldier who carries on fighting with blood pouring from a wound is almost certain to collapse – and be a danger to any comrades who try to rescue him. As for not seeking rest ... today, as I begin a two-week break from all duties (including diary-writing), I prefer to reflect on Jesus' words to the apostles when they were worn out after a tiring mission tour:

Come away to a deserted place all by yourselves and rest a while. (Mark 6:31)

♣ *Thursday 29 September*

Listen, I will tell you a mystery! (1 Corinthians 15:51)

St Paul is referring to the mystery of change from mortality to immortality, but his words could equally apply to the mysterious nature of the Universe and everything in it.

In case that's rather heavy for this time of the morning, afternoon or evening, let's pause for a game of *Family Fortunes*.

We asked 100 people what they associated with 'Michaelmas'. The top answer? 'Daisies!' It *should* have been the Feast of St Michael and All Angels (Anglican) or of Saints Michael, Gabriel and Raphael (Roman Catholic). It might not be advisable to go round on this day wishing everyone a 'Happy Michaelmas', unless you enjoy being compared to two items at our buffet tonight marking the occasion: crackers and fruitcake!

St Michael has been honoured as leader of the heavenly armies since the fourth century. In much of western Europe during the Middle Ages Michaelmas was a major religious feast coinciding with the harvest. Today it has all but disappeared in a society in love with e-mails, the internet and mobile phones with cameras, but which has all but lost the wider picture.

A few minutes in a library will reveal, for example, that the universe is around 13,000 million years old and contains at least 10^{11} star systems (galaxies), whilst the Earth is over 4.6 billion years old. On it, there are roughly one million trillion (10^{18}) insects alive at any given moment. Assuming 1 per cent of these are ants, the ants together have been calculated to weigh as much as all the humans!

Many people have become so bound up in the things of this world that they have little or no awareness that the Earth is only a fragment of God's creation: all that he has created in the beginning and is moving towards its ultimate fulfilment. As a country we are in danger of losing the insight that there are things which pass our understanding – that we are creatures of time and space, yet are destined for an eternal life with, and in, God. Without such a vision, no wonder many turn to the quirky, the peculiar, the strange and the eccentric and, in turn, become disillusioned, disappointed, dispirited and despairing. Belief in angels is not a rather quaint option giving comfort to the fanciful. It springs from an awareness that there is more to the universe than we can at present conceive, just as there is more to an iceberg than appears on the surface.

❧ *Friday 30 September*

There's a lot of interest in Bob Dylan, with the fortieth anniversary of the release of *Highway 61 Revisited*. To mark the occasion, we've adapted the words of 'The Times They Are A-Changin'' to fit the present position of the Church of England:

> Come gather round Anglicans,
> low church or near-Rome,
> and confess that you have been
> too prone to moan
> and accept you've let down
> him who died to atone;
> his love thought the world worth savin'.
> Then you'd better start lovin'
> or you'll sink like a stone –
> now the Church must be a-changin'.

In fact, there *are* signs that the Church is changing – becoming more welcoming to those who rarely, if ever, attend a formal service. Here at St Margaret's our biggest chance at present of reaching out in friendship is through Playtime, which today takes part in the World's Biggest Coffee Morning for the Macmillan Cancer Relief Appeal. Some of the mums have donated items towards the raffle. As always, there's a lot of laughter, and Bob Hoskins was right – it *is* good to talk! Playtime has made a marked difference to several new mothers, who would otherwise be isolated. Some parents taking part in Playtime decide after a while to attend our Family Service; others do not. That's as it should be. Our aim is not to 'bring people to Christ', but to bring something of Christ's love to people. How could we do otherwise, since he knows each one of them better even than we know ourselves?

October

❧ *Saturday 1 October*

'Hope springs eternal' – but if anyone is waiting for me to imitate the ladies doing aerobics on one of the new hall's springy floors, they could be here until Doomsday. In my view, the line in the hymn, 'Dance, then, wherever you may be' is rarely to be taken literally. Besides, when it comes to tripping the light fantastic, I have two left feet.

Today in the hall there is a follow-up to the parish mission day held in June. Being 'at home' is saving the cost of hiring the Clarke-Foley Centre but is not without problems – only a week after the opening, the lift is not working and the amplification is working overtime!

I put my cards on the table by saying we must move away from thinking about money to considering mission. If we are sure that the love of God shown in the death and Resurrection of Jesus is the world's ultimate hope, like the original Christians we must want to communicate that conviction; as the Swiss theologian Emil Brunner put it: 'The Church exists by mission as fire exists by burning.' St Margaret's is not a letting agency existing simply to pay off a loan. Our divinely appointed task is to wait on the love within the Holy Trinity and take something of it 'out there', bringing help and healing wherever we can. Sometimes this will involve mentioning our beliefs; more often, it will not. But as the wartime Archbishop William Temple remarked, the Church is 'the only organisation that exists primarily for the sake of those who are not its members'.

Several suggestions are made today about outreach, but the only positive step is the setting-up of a monthly Luncheon Club (which is unlikely, of course, to involve the under-30s). Whenever other ideas are put forward, the question is invariably, 'Who is going to do it?' Priests like myself will come and go, but if St Margaret's is to achieve its potential, everyone must be ready to say, with the prophet Isaiah: 'Here am I; send me!' (Isaiah 6:8). Hopefully today's meeting will at least have sown seeds from which growth will come.

❧ Sunday 2 October

There's a subtle change in emphasis to Harvest Festival these days. We still give thanks for the 'fruits of the earth', but the emphasis is increasingly on helping those in need in developing countries. 'Am I my brother's keeper?' asks Cain (Genesis 4:9). In today's global village, the answer must be 'Yes', which entails, with the Good Samaritan, not 'passing by on the other side' (Luke 10:29–37). So I'm delighted when special collections today raise £600 for the Leprosy Mission.

Leprosy (also known as Hansen's Disease) is a public health headache in 10 countries: Angola, Brazil, the Central African Republic, Congo, India, Liberia, Madagascar, Mozambique, Nepal and the United Republic of Tanzania. It is caused by a bacillus, and is probably spread through the air. If untreated, leprosy can cause disability, including blindness, by attacking nerves under the skin, leading to loss of feeling, paralysis and unfelt injury of the hands, feet and face. It is treatable through multi-drug therapy; more than 13 million people have been cured since the early 1980s, but over half a million new cases were detected in 2003 – more than 1,400 every day.

🌺 *Monday 3 October*

Thoughts of harvest lead naturally on to creation – for many still a stumbling-block and cause of religious doubt nearly 150 years after Charles Darwin published his *On the Origin of Species*.

Fundamentalists continually affirm their faith in the story of Genesis as opposed to the theory of evolution. But a close look at the opening chapters of Genesis shows that there is not *one* account of Creation, but *two*:

Genesis 1—2:4	Genesis 2:4–25
Day 1: Light – Day and Night	In the DAY the Lord God made the earth and heavens ... streams watered the ground ... man made from dust ... trees grow ... animals and birds ... woman made after man.

Day 2: Heaven
Day 3: Earth and vegetation,
             Seas
Day 4: Sun, moon, stars
Day 5: Water creatures, birds
Day 6: Cattle, reptiles, animals,
             Humanity (male and
             female)
Day 7: God rested

In the first (Genesis 1—2:4) life is created in six days, but in the second only one. In Genesis 1, man and woman are created together (v. 27), but in Genesis 2, woman is made from man's 'spare rib'.

Many theologians now consider that the author of Genesis 1 was using language *poetically* in praise of the Creator, because 'everything that he had made … was very good' (v. 31). The writer certainly did not write 'science', as we understand it – in his 'poem' day and night begin on Day 1, but the sun, moon and stars do not appear until Day 4! Textual analysis of the accounts has shown they were the produced by separate writers and combined later. The aim of the editor was not to give a *scientific* account of the origins of life but to introduce *religious* teaching in chapter 3 onwards about humanity's flawed condition and need of redemption. The greatness of God is contrasted with the fallibility of humanity, cut off from each other (Genesis 3 and 4) due to their estrangement from God, the source of life and love (the Hebrew word 'Adam' which is used as a personal name can equally mean 'a man' and 'mankind'). You don't have to look in the Bible for evidence about humanity's fallen condition. It stares out at you on every page of your newspaper except in the sports section, and sadly, these days it's often there as well.

One final point about creation. In all the apparently endless arguments between creationists and evolutionists, the emphasis is generally on the *process* ('how?'), not the *purpose* ('why?'). Christians should be much more ready to say *why* – because God is Love. The Almighty did not *need* to create (out of loneliness or boredom), since there exists within the Holy Trinity a community of love involving the Father, Son and Holy Spirit. But being perfect Love, God wanted to create beings capable of giving and receiving love, and his love overflowed in creation. I doubt whether the contrast between the vastness of God and his entire creation has ever been expressed better than by Julian of Norwich (*c.* 1342–1430) in her *Sixteen Revelations of Divine Love*:

> ... He shewed me a little thing, the quantity of a hazel nut, lying in the palm of my hand ... I looked thereupon and thought: 'What may this be?' And I was answered in a general way, thus: 'It is all that is made.' I marvelled how it could last, for methought it might fall suddenly to naught for littleness. And I was answered in my understanding: 'It lasts and ever shall last because God loves it, and so hath all-thing its being through the love of God.'

✌ *Wednesday 5 October*

BBC Radio Leeds reporter Spencer Stokes comes for an interview – presumably a 'catch-up' chat after my first six months at St Margaret's. I had been thinking of having a sabbatical from journalists, but poor Spencer has to eat. That doesn't mean I will listen to the interview when it is broadcast on the breakfast show. It's far too early in the morning to hear the sound of my own voice!

✌ *Thursday 6 October*

Every year the Diocesan Secretaries of the Church of England's Northern Province get together to discuss trade and generally gasbag. This year's meeting took place yesterday at the Craiglands Hotel, Ilkley. It was good to stand back from parish life for a while to exchange thoughts with like-minded people. When you're on a journey, it helps to check the route occasionally with fellow travellers.

❧ *Friday 7 October*

Just about everyone – apart from some contestants on TV quiz shows – knows about the feeding of the five thousand. Today I'm investigating a phenomenon which is not miraculous but still pretty amazing – the feeding with the five thousand.

I'm at the Froebelian School at Horsforth, Leeds, where the primary age pupils raised £5,562 in the last academic year through various events, including a ladies' night and sponsored walk of Yorkshire's Three Peaks – Ingleborough, Whernside and Pen-y-ghent. The money is going towards the Martin House Children's Hospice at Wetherby, of which I was Patron while Archbishop. Today the pupils hand me one of those huge cheques you see on Children in Need. It's a joy to pass it on to Stuart Andrews, head of fundraising at Martin House. The pupils are so enthusiastic and committed to this highly worthwhile cause.

One little girl involved in the presentation apparently told everyone the school was having a visit from 'The Pope of Ilkley'. That reminds me: I must ring my garage about the Hopemobile. Like many of those sad-looking people jogging round Ilkley on Sunday mornings, it would probably benefit from a service. Now – where did I put the Hope mobile?

❧ *Saturday 8 October*

It's 11 am in a cosy room at Christchurch, where St Margaret's member Maurice Mullard is introducing an eight-session course, 'Education for Global Justice'. Maurice is Professor of Social Policy at Hull University and has arranged the course as a follow-up to the G8 Summit at Gleneagles. With him is his colleague Simon Lee, Senior Lecturer in Politics, who has everyone in stitches with an anecdote of

how, as a student, he went to interview Tory Economics guru
Sir Keith Joseph at his London flat during the Thatcher years.
Sir Keith had not yet mastered his security system, and Simon
spent 20 minutes conducting the interview on the doorstep
while Mrs Thatcher's great friend remained inside!

Among those listening intently is LibDem activist James
Keeley, who is prominent in a bright pink shirt almost identi-
cal in colour to the top worn by his two-year-old daughter,
Alexandra, who is accompanied by her teddy and toy ele-
phant. The talk is on such important matters as 'The
International Finance Facility' and 'Inclusion or Ghetto-
isation?' but Alexandra has weightier matters on her mind.
She seems to be thinking: 'When is Gordon, the Fab
Controller, going to save the elephants in India from those
horrid ivory-hunters?'

Maurice, meanwhile, says that after the G8 summit anti-
poverty campaigners must concentrate on reform of world
financial institutions like the World Trade Organization,
International Monetary Fund and World Bank. In theory
they are run on a 'one nation, one vote' basis, yet poor countries cannot afford to send representatives to the almost-con-
stant finance meetings in Geneva, so the rich countries set the
agenda in their own interest. There should also be more open
government in the USA and EC, meetings between govern-
ments and business interests being minuted to cut the
influence on politicians from lobbies like those in the
pharmaceutical companies.

All this is rather above Alexandra's head – but she knows
the elephants are in safe hands. Many times at breakfast she
has heard her Daddy say nice things about Controller
Gordon's animal-loving friend, PC Tony. Only this morning,
he said (rather excitedly, she thought): 'Just when the country
needs that blessed man, he's off abroad again, bound for tusk
and knee.'

Elephants may not forget, but I obviously do – as is evident from an e-mail received by St Margaret's solving the mystery of the other David Hope (see 28 July). He currently directs two choirs in Ho Chi Minh City, Vietnam, but reminds me that we met while I was Vicar of All Saints', Margaret Street, London. Somewhere in England or Vietnam there's a photo of the two of us drinking beer in the church bar. We came across each other again several times when I was Bishop of Wakefield, since David belonged to Leeds Parish Church Choir and took part in several musical events in Yorkshire which I also attended.

In 2001 David went to Vietnam to run the Corporate Department of Ho Chi Minh City's largest provider of English language and management training. Vietnam has a sizeable (around 9–10 per cent) Christian minority, but since there is no Anglican presence in Vietnam he attends the Roman Catholic Notre Dame Cathedral and directs its choir, who sing in Vietnamese, English, Latin, French, German and Italian! The worshippers were delighted in 2003 when their Archbishop was created a Cardinal by Pope John Paul II.

David also directs the secular international choir, which performs for charities helping, amongst others, street children and disabled children. The members had to get permission to perform, and having waded through quantities of red tape were expecting a licence to arrive the day before a concert; in fact, it came next morning, only hours before the off!

So why the entry in our visitors' book? David says:

> In 2004 I read in a newspaper that Fr David was intending to retire as Archbishop and go to Ilkley. I have always had an interest in St Margaret's as one of my mother's best friends was Joan Wolstenholme (née Levesley) whose brother was Fr Tom Levesley [St Margaret's vicar from 1965 to 1980]. So I decided that

during my next UK visit I would attend St Margaret's.
I was staying with friends in Leeds, and drove over on
what turned out to be St Margaret's Patronal Festival. I
followed Mass with coffee at Betty's, which is a definite
'must' for me when visiting Ilkley! I'm rather a 'slipper-
away' in churches. I was happy to be at the Mass which
Fr David celebrated, and then to disappear without
bothering him – I don't like to make a fuss.

Next time the other David Hope visits Ilkley, we really must
have another photo taken!

✤ *Sunday 9 October*

'God speaks your language', reads a sign outside Christchurch, the Methodist-United Reformed church on The
Grove. Today the second language at St Margaret's is French,
owing to a visit to Ilkley by a party from Coutances, our twin
town in Normandy. The 10.30 am Solemn Eucharist has a
Gallic introduction when my welcome to the visitors is
translated impeccably into French by Monique Kershaw, a
member of the choir whose beautiful soprano solos have
added a certain *je ne sais quoi* to many services and concerts.

Translating French is '*un morceau de gâteau*' for Monique, a
Walloon, who has lived in England for half of her life. Monique
is a self-employed translator; she speaks French, German and
Dutch fluently, can get by in Italian and Spanish and has a
smattering of Danish. Talk about speaking in tongues –
Monique is like a concise version of the day of Pentecost!

By contrast, Mike Gibbons, Chairman of Ilkley Parish
Council, confesses that his French is 'absolutely diabolical'.
But he considers the language of friendship can overcome
linguistic differences – especially when translators are on hand
for speakers of both languages.

The link between Ilkley and Coutances, well known for its splendid cathedral, is now in its thirty-sixth year. Yves Lamy, Mayor of Coutances, here with his wife, Astrid, says the links that have developed between ordinary French and English people over the years are a witness to our common humanity – a positive sign in an often-troubled world.

Another welcome sign is our receipt of a letter starting 'Dear St Margaret's Church' from Mathilda, whom I christened in July. Besides our worship, she says she especially enjoyed helping to serve the coffee and attending open garden afternoons. 'I even got some recipes, one called Mathilda's Cake. I am now thinking of excuses to come to England and St Margaret's as soon as possible.'

The *entente* is clearly very *cordiale* within this *jeune fille charmante*!

After lunch today I conduct the third baptism here in as many days. I hope there isn't a water shortage on the way, in view of the healthy number of christenings here. I'm sure the PCC would object to any restrictions on our use of the font – although we are patriotic folk, we would not take kindly to suggestions that a five-inch line be painted on it, as in domestic baths during the war.

❧ Friday 14 October

My life is so busy that although I've been meaning to do so for some time, it's only today that I get round to visiting Ilkley Grammar School to meet the head teacher, Mrs Gillian James, an approachable and down-to-earth woman. Another Lancastrian – ah well, these people are sent to try us!

Despite its title, the 'grammar' school is a large comprehensive with an impressive record in the league table of results produced by the *Sunday Times*. After coffee with Gillian I am shown around by two teenage girls, who are enthusiastic about the opportunities available at the school. I sense a purposeful atmosphere and am impressed by the displays – especially those on the environment.

❧ *Saturday 15 October*

At Pentecost, the birthday of the Christian Church, St Peter declared that the outpouring of the Holy Spirit was the fulfilment of Joel's prophecy that 'old men shall dream dreams' (Acts 2:17). I'm sure Fr Richard Hoyal would not admit to being old; doubtless he'd quote the words immediately beforehand, 'young men shall see visions'. Either way, it's time to pay tribute to my predecessor. It was he who saw St Margaret's needed both a thriving Family Service and a parish hall for the new millennium, and who had the persistence (dare I say it: dog-gedness?) which enabled them to come into being.

Richard has a dry sense of humour, which grows on you like a fine wine. You wouldn't catch him using a catchphrase like the late Larry ('shut that door!') Grayson, a host of *The Generation Game*. Richard's last celebration of the Eucharist at St Margaret's was in February 2004, but a reminder of him is still visible in a note on the door leading downstairs to the vestry:

PLEASE KEEP SHUT
(DRAUGHTS! HEAVY GUTTERING
OF CANDLES!)
ESP. DURING SERVICES
(BUT NO NEED TO KEEP
LATCHING – NOISY!)

('Guttering' occurs when candle flames are caught by the breeze and the flame shoots upward, causing the wax to run.)

Today Richard and Muriel have a 'day off' – they're

obeying my three-line whip to come and open the new hall officially. First we've a Thanksgiving Eucharist, kept under the hour by the absence of a sermon (yes, they like that). Appropriately for 'the church by the moor', the Gospel includes the Beatitudes followed by Christ's call to 'Let your light shine before others' just as 'a city built on a hill cannot be hidden' (Matthew 5:1–16). Afterwards everyone heads for the hall, where the ladies have thoughtfully identified many items in the lavish buffet. One label reads 'mock crab' (most unwise to do so at Scarborough, though this crab is dead rather than quick). There's a large square cake with suitable words and a cross in gold – matching the curtain in front of the plaque which I ask Fr Richard and Muriel to uncover. Having had experience of this delicate task, I suggest they pull gently! Naturally I single them out in my thanks to many – the project would not have been possible without their inspiration, guidance and steadfastness. And it's amazing that the building has been completed on time, to budget, and to such a high standard – especially in the quality of the windows.

Richard recalls that when he first visited St Margaret's in 1989 to meet the churchwardens, Barbara France and Alan Brown, he could hardly believe his luck in coming to a church with such a fine organ and reredos where he might serve, 'if I played my cards right with Barbara'. But he felt 'bathos' on seeing a hall 'long past its sell-by date'. He goes on:

> Last night Barbara told me I would be 'gobsmacked' by the new building. Very little that happens in the Church of England surprises me these days but I conceded to Barbara when I saw the hall that I was pleased – very pleased. I trust you all will grab the opportunities to make the new hall a tremendous meeting place for all sorts of people.

As everyone is talking excitedly after the speeches, *Ilkley Gazette* photographer Adrian Murray arrives in the nick of time. He's been delayed because someone at the *Gazette* office left an instruction to go to St Margaret's Church – forgetting to specify Ilkley rather than Horsforth, Leeds, where he often works. Adrian gets Richard and Muriel to unveil the plaque again, and then requests a shot of the whole company – a tall order, you might think, with about 200 people chatting nineteen to the dozen. But Adrian has masterly people-management skills. In 2003 at the Harrogate première of *Calendar Girls* he climbed up a large stepladder and shouted to nearly 300 WI members enjoying a champagne reception: 'Right, girls – blouses!' 'Only you could have got away with it,' Adrian was told later by Jean MacQuarrie, the formidable but friendly editor-in-chief of Ackrill Newspapers, Harrogate. Today Adrian moves to the microphone and announces: 'If you'll all get your tickets out, I will draw the raffle shortly.' The ladies dive into their handbags and the gentlemen reach for their wallets. Suddenly there is something like the 'sound of sheer silence' felt by the prophet Elijah on Mount Horeb after his contest with the prophets of Baal (1 Kings 19:12). Adrian shepherds everyone to exactly where he wants and snaps away before anyone realises the raffle won't be drawn until our Christmas Fayre on 3 December.

✿ *Tuesday 18 October*

Today I take the funeral service of Joyce Garrett who died on Thursday aged 67 from cancer, only four days after I last saw her. Her faith helped her considerably, as Garth Kellett, who knew her much better than I did, testifies:

> When the Family Service started, Joyce and Greg and their daughters Susan and Ruth, together with their

families, began to come to St Margaret's regularly. Shortly afterwards Joyce and Ruth asked to be confirmed, and I led them up for confirmation by Martyn Jarrett, Bishop of Beverley.

Although Joyce's health continued to deteriorate, she rarely missed the Family Service. Her cheerful determination quite often masked the fact that she was seriously ill and in pain. Getting to church cost her a great deal, but her simple faith and infectious sense of humour were a delight to experience. She claimed to know little about the Church or religious things, but it was obvious that her straightforward trust in God and His love for her, along with her love for her family, gave her great strength and liveliness. She was the sort of person whose goodness leaves its footprints in our hearts.

❧ *Thursday 20 October*

St Margaret's has a growing – thriving almost – community of families with young children, but as yet we have made little impact with the 12–20 age group. The under-twenties, poor things, are bombarded by so many demands to conform. Determined to be different, they are persuaded by advertisers to buy the same mobile phones, clothes, music and magazines. In addition to this, peer pressure encourages thousands to put their health at risk through the same cigarettes and alcoholic drinks, and sometimes drugs.

How long is it before the young realise that Christianity is the real non-conformity, which enables people to be themselves in a world where people are pushed around, did they but know it, by large commercial organisations? St Paul caught the gist of the Christian's freedom when he wrote:

Do not be conformed to this world, but be transformed

by the renewing of your minds, so that you may discern
what is the will of God – what is good and acceptable
and perfect. (Romans 12:2)

There is no easy answer to my question – each congregation
will have its own ideas. But surely one positive step would be
to encourage teenage church members to enquire more
about their faith and to play a more active role in their particular church, thereby enabling them to be more effective
Christian ambassadors among their age range.

Adult churchgoers should be able to understand the young
even if we don't use their language (they wouldn't thank us for
patronising them). Forty years on Bob Dylan, like St Margaret's,
must seem hip-op rather than hip-hop to the under-twenties,
so today we've sneaked into the local organisations page of the
Ilkley Gazette what is probably the first rap poem to appear in
the paper since it was founded in 1861. We call it:

Parish Hall Rap

We've still 100 K needs raisin',
but we ain't fazin' –
grace is amazin'.
Gazin' at the hall,
we're sure it'll be paid for.
It's simply made for
exactly what you wanna do
(if it's not blue) –
we'll battle through.
Just keep on prayin's
what we're sayin'.
So come on down from 10 till 2,
on Saturday at St Margaret's Hall –
open 2U, open 4 all.

❧ Saturday 22 October

There's a steady stream of visitors to the new hall today, matching the rain which falls all morning. By 4 pm more than 100 people have toured the building, and quite a few have gone away with details of our hiring rates. Bookings are going well, and recent activities have included a baptism party, ruby wedding celebration, funeral tea and children's party.

❧ Sunday 23 October

Those of us old 'uns who are sometimes 'wearied by the changes and chances of this fleeting world' can leave church this morning feeling revived and with a spring in our steps, cheered up by Twinkletoes, four teenage girls from Ilkley Grammar School. George Herbert himself would rejoice at their attempts to introduce a bit of 'Heaven in ordinary'.

It's not just how the young are talking (as I mentioned the other day) but what they are saying, which includes at the moment 'Stand up for Africa'. Helena Beeson, Jenny Dybeck, Hollie Johnson and Gina Williams are hoping to collect £1,200 by next September to fund a farm in Africa through Oxfam. As mentioned in my diary entry of 2 July, they carried a banner displaying 56 African flags at the protest in Ilkley prior to the G8 summit. But let them speak for themselves:

GINA
Age: 13
Occupation: Eating, sleeping and doing fun stuff
Wouldn't leave the house without: A penny whistle and a battered old hat
Scared of: Things that go bump in the night
War or peace?: Peace. Any day. Oh yes ... a few days ago a

friend asked me, 'What the hell is war good for?' I replied cynically, 'Ridding Europe of fascism in the 1940s.'

Cats or dogs?: Birds!

Couldn't live without: Everything!

Most valued possession: My battered box of paint.

HOLLIE

Age: 13

Occupation: Student/part-time hippie

Wouldn't leave the house without: An open mind

Scared of: Orienteering. I *always* get lost!

War or peace?: Peace. Hippies rule!

Cats or dogs?: Catdogs.

Couldn't live without: Music

Most valued possession: My memory. What would I do without it?

JENNY

Age: 13

Occupation: Sleeping

Wouldn't leave the house without: Keys

Scared of: Chavs

War or peace?: Peace

Cats or dogs?: Cats. Dogs smell

Couldn't live without: Running

Most valued possession: My running shoes.

HELENA

Age: 13

Occupation: Schoolgirl

Wouldn't leave the house without: Clothes

Scared of: Spiders, dark and death

War or peace?: Peace

Cats or dogs?: Cats

Couldn't live without: Air

Most valued possession: If it can be a person, my dad. If not, num-num and blanco (a stuffed seal and stuffed bear I've had since I was about two days old).

The girls receive about £40 this morning, bringing their total up to around £100. They are planning to collect at schools, churches and other premises in Ilkley throughout the academic year, and have started their Twinkletoes Odd Jobs Service. Why 'Twinkletoes'? 'We had problems thinking of a name,' says Helena. 'It's just a name.'

❧ Tuesday 25 October

There's a priceless Northern saying – from Cumberland, I'm told – which runs: 'I'm all behind, like Mrs Brown's cow.' Rather colourful, you must admit (unless the cow is a Friesian) but not quite appropriate for adaptation at St Margaret's, where Father Brown's garden would probably only be big enough for a goat.

Anyway, life is getting busy again after the flat summer holiday period, and this entry is in fact being written a week or so after the date in question. As the guest of deputy churchwarden Allan Barnes I addressed the Rotary Club at the Craiglands (I'm still waiting for a discount in view of all the dinners I seem to attend there). As you would expect, I churned out all the usual stuff about the differences between my life 'then' and 'now'. What you're really wanting to know, however, is – did we have the fillet of beef or lamb? I'm afraid I can't remember now. But in any case it wouldn't do to mention the word 'beef' in the hearing of a VIP I'm dining with tomorrow!

❧ *Wednesday 26 October*

I felt rather sorry for John Selwyn Gummer when he was savaged by the media after giving a beefburger to his four-year-old daughter Cordelia at the height of the (media-induced) BSE panic in 1990. I bet that in the absence of a gimmick they wouldn't have given much space to the Agriculture Ministry's view. I wonder what else would have satisfied them? Perhaps something guaranteeing a good feed for the press beforehand – maybe even steak and chips.

Today the Ritz is playing it safe at the *Country Life/Strutt and Parker* lunch at which Britain's favourite market town will be chosen. There's not a scrap of beef in sight, as we tuck into:

> Sauté of sea scallops with confit of potatoes and
>   chorizo salad
> Roast breast of partridge with chestnuts and
>   grapes, cep and lemon verbena sauce
> Ensemble of passion fruit
> Coffee or tea
> Petit fours

Quality, yes, but perhaps slightly lacking in quantity – though of course in today's health-conscious climate many people prefer not to over-indulge at lunchtime, and anyone still hungry afterwards can always fill up with what they call in the West Riding 'a slice of jam and bread'.

During the meal the regional judges speak in turn for five minutes on behalf of their top town, after which the editor of *Country Life* referees a battle between them. It comes down to either John Gummer or me in the end, and apparently my presentation is more robust so Hexham gets the glory. I'm happy to settle for six bottles of fine French wine! A word in conclusion to my fellow judges, the sponsors and everyone at the Ritz – 'Santé!'

✣ *Sunday 30 October*

So it's official: sunbathing is good for you – and you can do as much of it as you like!

The advice comes from the highest authority on the subject in the land – Rowan Williams, Archbishop of Canterbury. He's not talking about *physical* sunbathing, which is not his cup of tea. What a relief: if a piece of glass was lying about, that famous beard might burst into flames, and he's supposed to set others on fire, not himself! No, Dr Williams has likened prayer to sunbathing: both involve resting in the light and letting it come in. To George Herbert, prayer is a channel enabling us to draw on the divine energy, since it is:

> … the Churche's banquet, Angels' age,
> God's breath in man returning to his birth …

Today we mark All Saints-tide (two days before All Saints Day itself), when we give thanks for those who have walked abundantly 'in the light', the 'official' saints. People like St Peter and St Paul, but also some other weird and wonderful characters like St Wilfrid the Elder (634–709). Because he thought he wouldn't get a 'proper' ordination as bishop in England, Wilfrid went to France to be sure of a legitimate consecration. Then there was Augustine, who certainly knew how to sin (and sin well!) and rather enjoyed it. Despite their 'good as gold' image, the saints were human like us. They were sinful, wayward, weak, useless – wicked in some cases. Their lives were transformed not by their own efforts but by the mercy and grace of God to become more truly the human persons they were created to be, thereby reflecting all the more perfectly that image and likeness of God in which each of us is made. We, too, can be changed.

But the New Testament knows nothing at all of such saints,

even though the word appears frequently, especially in St Paul's letters to the earliest Christian communities. He writes to the 'saints' in Corinth, Rome, Philippi, and so on: saint is the New Testament equivalent of 'Christian'. I am not suggesting we go round calling each other St David, St Alan or St Barbara, but the grace of God which comes through baptism and following Christ ought to make a difference – we ought to be recognised as people who prefer not to be served but to serve. It is often through daily small acts of kindness, mercy, compassion and generosity that God's will is being done on Earth as it is in Heaven. It won't happen simply because you and I make an effort (though that must remain a part of it). No – it'll come through being close to the Light of the world.

November

✣ Tuesday 1 November
ALL SAINTS' DAY

However eccentric your vicar may be, (s)he will not be in the same league as St Simeon the Younger (*c.* AD 521–597), called Stylites ('*stylos*', 'pillar' [Greek]), a monk who spent his last 45 years (give or take a few) upon a pillar on the Hill of Wonders, near Antioch, Syria. *The Guinness Book of Records* (1984 edition) says: 'This is probably the earliest example of record setting.' Few details of the saint's achievement survive, although it is known that at night he regularly dropped off.

✣ Wednesday 2 November
ALL SOULS' DAY

> And therefore never send to know for whom the bell tolls; It tolls for thee. (John Donne)

And me. For in church tonight, on All Souls Day, there is no escape from the underlying theme – death. Yet as always when Christians meet, there is the assurance of Christ's resurrection victory – our ultimate hope. The mood is sombre as the names of family and friends who have gone ahead of us are read out – a duty which takes Fr Alan Brown more than six minutes. Yet it helps to meditate afresh on the nature of the Church. At its heart, it is not a social and/or political organisation. It is a community of the faithful – both those living and those even more alive in the nearer presence of God.

Dominating the service tonight is Fauré's Requiem, in which the choir are accompanied by the organist Christian Spence, our director of music. A loud, deep note on the organ leads into the choir's solemn introduction:

> *Requiem aeternam dona eis Domine.*
> (Rest eternal grant to them, O Lord.)

There is a sense of awe (in its real meaning) right up to the sublime climax:

> *In paradisum deducant te angeli ...*
> (May the angels lead you into paradise ...)

when it seems that, by a tiny effort of the will, we could float through the celestial gates to join that greater company in Heaven. As usual during the Eucharist, we are in the presence of a great and wonderful mystery. Fr Alan Brown says only a brief homily for, he says:

> If we listen to the words of the Mass carefully, there is really no need of a sermon, save to say, 'Let us thank God for having known those whom we remember this night and shall do in succeeding days as we carry on in our earthly pilgrimage – and let us look forward to that day when we too are in that closer presence of God.'

❧ *Saturday 5 November*

Oyez, oyez, oh ... shut up – there's only one town crier, and today he's in Ilkley's central square drumming up support for the Wharfedale Naturalists Society, which is holding a coffee morning at 10 am before an exhibition in the afternoon marking its sixtieth anniversary. Chris Richards is keen to stress that the organisers are naturalists, not naturists. 'It's far too cold for *that*,' he says, as a chill autumn wind blows through the square.

Anyone within a quarter of a mile who can't hear Chris should perhaps inquire about one of those 'miracle hearing aids' featured in the weekend colour supplements. For their benefit and yours, his message is:

> Oyez! Oyez! Oyez!
> A coffee morning is happening
> at the Clarke-Foley Centre today.
> It's being run by the Wharfedale Naturalists –
> it's their Jubilee, so they say.
> You could buy a home-made cake,
> a jar of jam or two,
> some Christmas cards, a plant or book –
> I'll leave it up to you.
> It's going on from ten till noon,
> so hurry along, and get there soon.
> God save the Queen!

Chris often helps good causes for a token present rather than money; today he receives 'a few' cans of beer. I wonder …

Tonight (as an alternative to fireworks) there's another fine concert of music and poetry organised by Nadine Wharton in aid of Traidcraft. It's entertaining and stimulating – you couldn't possibly fall asleep, and I must not! There's a fair turn-out of around 65, and the evening fetches a healthy £233.15. Charity may begin at home, but doesn't remain there at St Margaret's – even though we still need nearly £100,000 for our new parish hall. Around £600 has also been collected for relief work in the Kashmir region following the recent earthquake.

❧ *Sunday 6 November*

> A man that looks on glasse,
> On it may stay his eye;
> Or if he pleaseth, through it passe,
> And then the heav'n espie.
>
> (George Herbert, The Elixer)

We are looking on glass this morning – just as Alice did at the start of *Through the Looking Glass* – as I dedicate a stained-glass window at the church's west end. It's an old window, *The Christ with the Doctors of Law*, made around 1911 for Dunstable Priory. It was saved by the London Stained Glass Repository and installed here in May 2004 to the glory of God and in memory of the donor's parents.

The window pictures the moment (Luke 2:41–52) when the 12-year-old Jesus was discovered by Mary and Joseph in the Temple at Jerusalem after he had wandered away from his family. Today we are joined by the restorer, Keith Barley, of York, and David Ingmire, representing the Glaziers Company and the Repository.

The idea of penetrating into another world more fulfilling than this one is recurrent. Unless you are a recluse, you will be aware that Hogwart's School of Witchcraft and Wizardry is reached via the magical platform 9¾ at King's Cross Station, while Narnia is reached through an apparently ordinary wardrobe.

A sceptical generation like ours finds it hard to imagine how you can 'pass through the glass', as George Herbert suggests. In fact, it is much easier than might appear at first sight. You just need to play 'Follow My Leader' – following Jesus, who went through the divide *the other way* and is now and for ever a bridge between time and eternity.

George Herbert is suggesting that God is much more

accessible than he appears on the surface. He says the Lord makes himself known through ordinary substances like water, bread and wine. There is nothing remarkable about water in the font – until it is made special by God's Holy Spirit, who can give everyone the 'living water' promised by Jesus to a Samaritan woman (John 4:1–42). Similarly, the bread and wine on the altar, when blessed, offer a foretaste of Heaven here on Earth through contact with Jesus, the Living Bread. Prayer and Bible-reading are other means by which God can give us glimpses into Heaven now.

Perhaps your spiritual wardrobe is cluttered with ideas absorbed from popular culture, including the idea that Heaven is remote from this world – or even non-existent. Who says so? Other people! Your life is not theirs, and you are free to investigate whether George Herbert is right. The way through the glass divide may be easier than you think.

❧ Thursday 10 November

A visit to the Quaker-controlled Ackworth School, Pontefract, to address about 150 members of the sixth form on 'The Spiritual Journey' as part of a Religious Studies module.

Christians have had widely differing religious experiences down the centuries. Some people (like St Paul) can give the date and even the hour of their conversion – so sudden and dramatic has it apparently been. Others claim no sudden moment of illumination. There can hardly be a statement of faith with more reservations than that by Dag Hammarskjöld, UN Secretary-General (1953–61):

> I don't know who – or what – put the question, I don't know when it was put. I don't even remember answering. But at some moment I did answer 'yes' to Someone – or Something – and from that hour I was

certain that existence is meaningful and that, therefore, my life in self-surrender had a goal. From that moment I have known what it means 'not to look back', and 'to take no thought for the morrow'.

St John of the Cross' notion of 'the dark night of the soul' reflects the fact that a few people exist in a kind of fog – allied, sometimes, to mental anguish.

My message to the young? Stick at it – keep asking questions, and don't be deterred if the answers are slow in coming about, or from, God. Others will have been down your road before you, and God will be there somewhere in your quest for enlightenment. No wonder the early Church was called 'the Way' (Acts 9:2), rather than 'the Destination'. Even St Paul, despite the spectacular vision granted to him, only claimed to know 'in part' (1 Corinthians 13:9).

❧ Sunday 13 November

One of my predecessors as Bishop of Wakefield – in fact, the first bishop – was William Walsham How, writer of the hymn, 'For all the saints'. Concerned at the spiritual sleepiness in parts of the Diocese, he encouraged churches to say Holy Communion early on Sundays. In one parish he met an elderly verger, who was deaf and spoke loudly. When the old man brought up the plate, he shouted to the celebrant: 'There's eight on 'em 'ere , but two hasn't paid.'

As the Preacher in Ecclesiastes put it, 'there is nothing new under the sun' (Ecclesiastes 1:9). Churches are struggling with considerable demands on their resources. Faced by these difficulties, what should our response be? Today I suggest in the sermon that we should continually reflect on the nature of God, the giver of all life, who loved his world so much that he gave his only Son, Jesus Christ – to the point of death.

God's very nature is about giving and sharing. To come down to earth, we all know that inflation rises annually. We need to ensure we keep our giving at least in line with inflation. Many churches embrace the biblical principle of tithing. Perhaps we should do so at St Margaret's?

But on Remembrance Sunday we cannot think only about the giving of money. It is time again to be thankful for all those, known and unknown, who were ready to sacrifice themselves for our freedom. So often it takes a great disaster to bring the peoples of the world to their senses, to work together for the common good. We too ought to be prepared to give and to share. As St Francis of Assisi said: 'It is in giving that we receive ... in dying that we are born into eternal life.'

🔖 *Monday 14 November*

Children doubting the existence of Santa Claus can bid their anxious fears subside at our Christmas Fayre. They may tug his beard and find it genuine – just as the apostles were allowed to examine Jesus' hands and feet on the first Easter Sunday. On Saturday 3 December Santa is to make probably the first of his many appearances in this area at the Clarke-Foley Centre. Our social committee chose the venue because our new hall will not be known sufficiently by the regulars attending Saturday morning events in Ilkley.

Santa's visit has been arranged by former nurse Bill Godfrey (72), who is very close to the genial old fellow – and who, by coincidence, is bearded himself. Bill has been involved in amateur dramatics for more than 50 years, and in 2001 wrote and directed *The Real Santa Claus* which was performed by parishioners in church on St Nicholas' Eve, 5 December. It was placed on the internet and is, as I write, still available via www.stnicholascenter.org.

The story of Santa Claus developed from that of the real-life St Nicholas, who was born into a rich merchant's family in what is now south-eastern Turkey in the fourth century. He inherited considerable wealth at the age of 15 when his parents died, but gave it all away to enter a monastery and train as a priest.

Bill says:

> Every country has a different name for him – Hagios Nikolaios in Greece, San Nicola in Italy and Sinte Klaas in Holland. When Dutch Protestants emigrated to America early in the seventeenth century, the Sinte Klaas festival went with them. Mixed with a bit of Scandinavian mythology, by the start of the nineteenth century 'Sinte Klaas' had become 'Santa Claus'. Poor old Saint Nicholas got lost in Britain's new commercial Christmas, but we still remember him every year on 6 December.

✺ *Tuesday 15 November*

Whatever problems each new generation has to face, it has the consolation of discovering the Revd Sydney Smith, the Canon of St Paul's, who must rank high in the list of great British wits.

Who else could be introduced to a woman at dinner and say moments later:

> Madam, I have been looking for a person who disliked gravy all my life; let us swear eternal friendship.

His many gems include:

> I am just going to pray for you at St Paul's, but with no very lively hope of success.

and:

> As the French say, there are three sexes – men, women,
> and clergymen.

(I suppose there are four today, following the ordination of
women to the priesthood!)

Tonight I am at Oliver's Paris Restaurant and Bar, Leeds,
for a pre-Christmas dinner arranged by the Bradford Organists Association. It's a strange occasion, as we haven't a room
to ourselves and several non-organists are earwigging as I get
up to speak. I crack a few jokes, and as no one says: 'Pipe
down!', I butter 'em up by saying organists are indispensable
to churches (as they are, of course). Then comes my *coup de
grace* – a great Smith simile:

> Organists are like carthorses: they always want more
> wind and another stop.

✣ *Wednesday 16 November*

Today I'm at Lambeth Palace, not to visit the Archbishop but
to present the Religious Radio Awards 2005 from the
Sandford St Martin Trust, which promotes excellence in religious broadcasting.

The £2,000 first prize goes to Premier Christian Radio for
its programme *The Rainbow Through the Rain*, telling the story
of Geoffrey Mowat's experiences as a prisoner of the Japanese
during the Second World War, which influenced his decision
to be ordained. It's a special pleasure to make the award since
I attended the launch of Premier Christian Radio as Bishop
of London in 1995.

Good radio programmes probably have far more impact –
and reach many more people – than any church sermon. Her

presence may have been inconvenient at times, but I really did welcome and value those visits to St Margaret's in March by the lady with the mic, Radio 4 producer, Sarah Lewthwaite.

❧ Thursday 17 November

'Give us this day our daily bread.' You have almost certainly seen one of those adverts for sliced bread with snapshots of supposed Northern life in 'the good old days' and voices in the background telling you to buy Hovis, Warburtons or some other 'good old-fashioned real bread'.

Today another slogan from the past comes to mind – 'I'm the mother in Mother's Pride: they named it after me!' – when I am at York Minster as one of four recipients of an Honorary Fellowship from York St John College. Mine is presented by the acting chair of the governors, David Smith, the former Bishop of Bradford, whom I know well.

As Archbishop of York I was part of the College's governing body, and in 2004 the College renamed its RE Centre after me. I have a few of these fellowships, and people are kind in thinking of me, but usually I put the scrolls away in a drawer and forget about them. *Sic transit gloria mundi* – 'so passes earthly glory'. Any gifts of mine were mainly received – either through genes, God's grace, or the influence of others – and I'm quite content where I am now in the service of the risen Lord Jesus, who was dearly loved for his obedience to the point of death – in fact, his Father's Pride!

❧ Sunday 20 November

Today is Stir-Up Sunday, when a long-standing Anglican prayer begins, 'Stir up, O Lord, the wills of your faithful people …' I wonder how many housewives down the years have listened beyond the first four words of this plea for enthusiasm, because the Collect before Advent has long been a signal that this is the day for making Christmas puddings and cakes. No such distraction for parishioner Mrs Sarah Williams, who after a visit to London on Thursday came home with a top-of-the-range Christmas pudding from Fortnum and Mason. 'I have never made a cake in my life,' she confesses. 'Around 10 years ago I bought all the ingredients from Booths in Ilkley – and they are still on my shelves. Once I made some buns for my children, but they tasted like scrambled egg.'

❧ Monday 21 November

If you have visited York Minster, you will be familiar with the great Five Sisters Window, and if you are a culture vulture you'll at least have heard of Chekhov's play *The Three Sisters*. Let me now introduce you to Ilkley's theatrical two sisters.

You have already come across Lay Reader Catherine Gibson, who starred in *Rough Justice* at Ilkley Playhouse in April. Catherine was Librarian at Ilkley College for 22 years before taking early retirement to train as a Reader, being licensed to St Margaret's in 2001. Her sister Vanessa works in marketing with Yorkshire Arts and Business, a company linking the business and arts worlds. Vanessa acted professionally for a while but developed an interest in directing while at Oxford University. This week she is the director of *Macbeth* at Ilkley Playhouse, where Catherine is prompter.

The cast only totals eight, as several people are taking two or more roles. Lady Macbeth is played by former Playtime mum Alison McKeefry, while another parishioner, Simon Waley, is Banquo, Murderer and Doctor. The play is fairly well received by the *Ilkley Gazette*, and is enjoyed by several St Margaret's members – although they disagree with the *Gazette* critic's comment that Alison is dressed 'like an extra from *Calendar Girls*'. One red-blooded male reports that red-haired Alison looks very attractive barefoot in a 'tasteful' nightie during the famous sleep-walking scene, gripping the audience while making hand-washing movements with a glazed look in her eyes.

No comments, please, about *Calendar Girl* calendars at St Margaret's. I am sure that the idea, like Lady Macbeth's hands, just would not wash with our ladies.

❧ *Friday 25 November*

Today I am at Cottingley Village Primary School, Bradford, surrounded by children involved in activities such as balloon-modelling, dance and puppet workshops and face-painting.

I'm representing the Bishop at a local fundraising day to help the last push for funds before work begins in March on a £4.8 million scheme aimed at revitalising the centre of Cottingley, an outer area of Bradford left behind by other local regeneration initiatives. The other guests include Philip Davies, MP for Shipley; Fiona Ellis, a Trustee of Future-builders England, who have given over £1 million to the project; and Councillor Simon Cooke, Bradford Council's deputy leader.

The Cottingley Cornerstone Centre scheme is led by St Michael's PCC and the Diocese of Bradford, helped by a large number of local individuals and organisations. Bradford Metropolitan District Council, the Saltaire GP practice and North Bradford Primary Care Trust have been vital partners, while Prince Charles has been involved through the Prince's Foundation for Architecture, making a personal donation to demonstrate his commitment to the project.

The original church was demolished in 2003 after being condemned as dangerous. The new centre will provide facilities including a new church, hall, IT room, GP surgery, pre-school nursery, elderly day-care area, youth room, respite care area for young disabled people, plus an arts and crafts room. There will be 52 affordable homes for sale.

What is really exciting – and augurs well for the project's success – is that it will benefit those who made it happen; the Centre's chair, Canon Sue Pinnington, describes it as 'regeneration from the bottom up'. Sue, Vicar of Cottingley since 2000, was a community and youth worker in the Midlands and an administrator for the Church Commissioners before her ordination. Her work with Cornerstone must leave little time for her leisure activities, which I am told include watercolour painting. I am not sure if that includes face-painting, but don't stop to ask!

❧ Saturday 26 November

The darkness of a late autumn afternoon is dispelled at 5 pm when Sir Jimmy Savile, who lives in Leeds, switches on Ilkley's Christmas lights for the second time following his earlier visit to the town in 2001. One of the lights has already been on for about a fortnight, and a PCC member wryly suggests it will now go out and stay out.

Inside St Margaret's at 6 pm, the only light is from a single candle in the nave, and a bulb at the east end allowing the choir to process in and Christian Spence to read his organ music. The season of green, Trinity, is drawing to a close on what for the Church is New Year's Eve. The clergy are robed in purple and Philippa Higgins is wearing a purple coat and new purple hat – bringing her collection up to 33.

When everyone is in place, the silence is broken by an Introit sung to music from a setting of the Magnificat by Palestrina. It awakens genuine awe when swirling around the vastness of York Minster, and the helpful acoustics in St Margaret's make the choir's marvellous, unaccompanied singing special too:

> I look from afar, and lo, I see the power of God com-
> ing and a cloud covering the whole earth. Go ye out to
> meet him and say: Tell us, art thou he that should come
> to reign over thy people Israel ... ?

As the choir sing the hymn 'Creator of the Stars of Night',
more than 200 candles protected by cardboard shields are lit,
from one to the next. I say a prayer of penitence for those sins
which hinder the coming of God's reign of love for the whole
human family, ending with:

> May he guide us into the way of peace, give light to
> those who sit in darkness and the shadow of death, and
> kindle in us the fire of his love.

There are still four Sundays before Christmas, but already
there is a sense of expectancy and wonder at the approaching
mystery of Christ's Incarnation – conveyed in the magnificent
anthem, 'A Spotless Rose' (fourteenth century/Howells):

> A spotless rose is blowing,
> sprung from a tender root of ancient seers'
>   foreshowing,
> of Jesse promised fruit;
> its fairest bud unfolds to light
> amid the cold, cold winter,
> and in the dark midnight.
> The rose which I am singing,
> whereof Isaiah said,
> is from its sweet root springing
> in Mary, purest Maid;
> for through our God's great love and might,
> the Blessed Babe she bare us
> in a cold, cold winter's night.

Alzheimer's victim Trevor Hearnshaw has heard the anthem
many times since he came to Ilkley with Pam in 1972. The
intellectual part of his brain has gone, but his emotional side
continues and he insists on humming during this and the
choir's other unaccompanied works. Pam tries gently to
quieten him but is only slightly embarrassed – friends are all
around. It may not appear so on the surface, but I am sure that
ultimately Trevor will be safe within that 'great love and
might' – as indeed will those shivering beneath the snows of
Kashmir who have not yet received our help following the
recent earthquake.

✤ *Sunday 27 November*
ADVENT SUNDAY

How is Christianity to be advanced in Britain's multicultural,
secular society in which there is widespread misunderstand-
ing – ignorance even – about the beliefs expressed in the
creeds, our basic statements of faith?

Fr Alan Brown, today's preacher, has been discussing this
problem with David Smith, the previous Bishop of Bradford,
who suggests we look beyond immediate concerns about
church attendances and finance to the heart of the matter.
Bishop David considers the Church needs to be built up and
see itself as a 'community of forgiveness, compassion, hope
and faith' – and to take these qualities into an often deeply
troubled world. This is in keeping with Christ's description of
his followers as the 'salt of the earth' (Matthew 5:13) for, as
every good cook knows, salt is not to be valued for itself but
for its ability to bring to life what might otherwise lack that
special flavour.

'In the run-up to Christmas, we would all do well to think
beyond our walls – and our shores even – to Africa and other
places where there is poverty and great need,' says Alan.

🎵 *Tuesday 29 November*

If you like classical music, you are probably familiar with Vaughan Williams' *The Lark Ascending*, that wonderful piece for the violin – especially if you are addicted to Classic FM, who play it so often that the lark must have a nesting-box at the radio station.

Today I'm up before the lazy lark in time to catch the 0609 from Ilkley – the only train to take if you must be on the 0720 from Leeds to King's Cross. I've an important tête-à-tête lined up with a charming, intelligent and attractive woman – just me and a few (hundred thousand) others who will tune in next month to hear us chatting on *Desert Island Discs*.

Sue Lawley is natural and relaxed during our meeting – the complete professional. We talk for a while before the recording to give her some background material, and that's it. In we go to the room with the green light, Sue with stopwatch (2½ minutes for each selection) and me (fortunately!) with no need of make-up – radio is much more relaxing for interviewees than TV.

Sue is particularly interested in how my 'big sister', cousin Muriel, introduced Anne and me to High Anglicanism at Wakefield Cathedral. The whole programme is done in a single take, enabling me to be on the midday train back home.

My eight Desert Island Discs are:

> Mozart's Symphony no. 40
> 'The Floral Dance' (Grimethorpe Colliery Band)
> *O Ce Veste Minunate* (O Wonderful Tidings,
>   traditional Romanian carol)
> Sanctus from Bach's Mass in B Minor
> 'On Ilkley Moor Baht 'At' (Black Dyke Mills Band)
> 'Land of the Mountain and the Flood'
>   (Hamish MacCunn)

188BETTER TO TRAVEL HOPEFULLY

'Lift Thine Eyes to the Mountains' from Mendelssohn's
Elijah
Part of Rachmaninov's Vespers

Mozart's Symphony no. 40 is an obvious starter, since it was
the first record I heard in the front room at home on our old,
wind-up gramophone. The Grimethorpe Colliery Band playing 'The Floral Dance', as brass bands are such a part of
Yorkshire culture. The Romanian carol reminds me of my
time as a parish priest in Romania in 1967–68, when I was
struck by the vibrancy and courage of the Church in the face
of an oppressive Communist régime under Ceaucescu. I
could hardly *not* have chosen 'On Ilkla Moor Baht 'At', and I
picked the Hamish MacCunn because each summer I escape
to the far north of Scotland.

Sue rules out the Complete Works of Dickens as my
'book', so I pick *The Pickwick Papers* – largely because the
account of the Eatanswill Election is so hilarious. My 'luxury'
is a case of selected malt whiskies. It would probably last a
good while, since I should only have a small tot now and
again. Once it was finished, I should draw on the Holy Spirit,
who of course will never run out.

❧ *Wednesday 30 November*

Walking down Wells Road to St Margaret's this morning, I
nearly come a cropper and clutch a wall for support. No, I
didn't overdo it last night – it's icy, and the surfaces of both
roads and pavements are treacherous. I fare better than nine
local children, who are carried to safety through a smashed
windscreen after the minibus taking them to school overturns
on black ice.

Naturally, the youngsters are in our prayers at an evening
Eucharist remembering fisherman St Andrew, the brother of

St Peter, whom he introduced to Jesus. The prayers are centred round the Church and people in Scotland, and we also
think of the missions to seamen throughout the world.

Saint Andrew's body is reputed to lie in the crypt of Amalfi
Cathedral, near Sorrento in Italy. According to a late (not
entirely reliable) tradition, St Peter's brother was martyred at
Patras in southern Greece in AD 60. An early medieval forgery
attributed to St Andrew the founding of the church in
Constantinople, to which his relics were later said to have
been taken. During the Middle Ages, crusaders reputedly
moved them to Amalfi. The cathedral contains a majestic
bronze statue of the saint by Michelangelo Naccherino
weighing about 8 cwt, while behind the altar, by contrast, is a
painting of an elderly, broad and strong bearded man nailed to
an X-shaped cross.

According to one legend, St Andrew journeyed to Scotland
and stayed at what is now St Andrews in Fife. St Andrew's
cross, which represents Scotland on the Union flag, was
associated with the saint from the tenth century onwards. I
don't suppose many of those waving Scottish or Union flags
at sporting fixtures often stop to think they are holding
high the representation of an instrument of torture. How
magnetic Jesus' personality must have been for those first
disciples to have obeyed the call to 'follow me' in both life and
death!

I hope that the nine children caught up in today's accident
will have many happy days to come once they have got over
the shock. No one can escape from suffering in a world of
change and decay – but you will appreciate the comforting
thought behind 'Abide with Me'. How wise of Mrs C. F.
Alexander, the writer of 'Once in Royal David's City' to have
included in 'Jesus Calls Us', her hymn for St Andrew's Day, the
lines:

In our joys and in our sorrows,
days of toil and hours of ease,
still he calls, in cares and pleasures,
'Christian, love me more than these.'

❧ WINTER –

Let Them Eat Haggis

December

🍂 *Saturday 3 December*

It's just before 10 am, and Santa is a little ... not cross or grumpy – perhaps 'saddened' is the word I want. He's come a fair distance from his home (at least 400 yards) and was rather hoping he would be offered his own dressing room at the Clarke-Foley Day Centre, where our Christmas Fayre is about to begin. After all, he is a Lapp of honour.

Instead, the only spare room in the centre has been allocated to 22 young ladies from Ilkley Dance Academy, who have sportingly agreed to put on a display at 11 am. They have been working hard: their instructor, Heather Holt, has been going through the routines with them since September.

Being a gentleman of the old school, Santa (alias Bill Godfrey) is in fact pleased to help the younger generation and doesn't mind robing in his grotto (armchair to you and me). His mind is really on that trim he's been planning to treat his full beard to after agreeing a few months ago to fit us into his busy winter schedule. In the meantime, he's enjoying the company of his little helpers, May Hughes (nine) and her sister Elizabeth (eight), supervised by senior pixie Kim Brooke (24).

Across the hall underneath the stage, Lesley Ayres is getting her bric-a-brac stall ready. She's here slightly later than planned: the London taxi she bought from Carlisle via eBay in September was 'a bit poorly' this morning, so she had to come in her Maxi.

Santa and the dancers are making their debut at the

Christmas Fayre, while the new holiday souvenir stall replaces the white elephant.

The dancers and their mums start arriving at 10.15 am, and seem to keep on coming – like the 'ever-rolling stream' mentioned in 'O God, Our Help in Ages Past'. They're keyed up and give a terrific show, dancing to Christmas pop music. Santa is slightly disappointed at the number of his visitors – around 20 – but it's not bad for a first visit. Business has been brisk at the holiday souvenir stall, and the tombola has been a great success. I didn't win the whisky this time – just two bottles of wine.

☙ *Sunday 4 December*

Barbara France has done her sums and says the fair has netted over £1,000. A tidy sum – didn't we do well! (Yes, Brucey kindly sent a signed photo for the 2002 celebrity auction inscribed, 'Whatever you paid for this, I hope it was worth it!')

A sign that Christmas is on the way will be the publication on Thursday of our quarterly parish magazine, to be delivered free to houses throughout the parish by volunteers – 'you, you and you'! It's a slimmed-down version of the normal magazine and gives a flavour of the spirit at St Margaret's in addition to details of Christmas services.

An advert is to go in the *Gazette* on Thursday announcing that a 'mystery fun guest' joins us next Sunday for our Christingle Service in aid of the Children's Society. No peeping ahead seven days!

☙ *Thursday 8 December*

It's getting busier as Christmas approaches – the PCC met on Tuesday, and this week there are plenty of people to see in and around the parish. A pleasant break today, though, when I'm

invited to a lunch which Bishop David James puts on at
Bishopscroft: ' … he gave gifts to his people' (Ephesians 4:8).
Among the talents received by David is clearly cooking, since
he makes a pretty mean beef casserole.

🐟 *Saturday 10 December*

Carols at the bandstand after lunch, organised by Churches
Together in Ilkley. It's encouraging to see several local schools
providing musicians and singers. As well as all the parents,
there are plenty of bystanders wondering what it's all about.
I'm the compere, and give a short talk about the Christmas
story. Mulled wine and mince pies afterwards – I do recommend waiting on the Lord as well as gaining weight at
Christmas!

It's *Messiah* time again, and the church is full almost to
capacity for a splendid performance of Handel's masterpiece
by four visiting soloists with Cantores Olicanae and the Ilkley
Sinfonietta.

If anyone thinks Christmas is only for children – a nice
story about a baby ('let him stay in the manger – don't let him
grow up'), Handel dispels that illusion at the opening of Part
Two, when he summarises Christianity in a nutshell:

> Behold the Lamb of God, that taketh away the sin of
> the world.

Followed almost immediately by:

> He was wounded for our transgressions,
> He was bruised for our iniquities …
> And with His stripes we are healed.

Reminding us of humanity's flawed condition are several local members of Amnesty International, which is running its annual campaign at Christmas asking people to send cards to victims of human rights violations and their defenders. In the busy-ness of our daily lives it's hard to remember the prisoners of conscience. Are those of us in Britain who 'confess the faith of Christ crucified' (comfortable in our cosy beds and churches), rather like those rebuked in the sleeping church in Sardis (Revelation 3:1–6)? There's no mistaking the menace lurking behind advice from Amnesty to those proposing to send Christian cards:

> Only send religious cards when recommended, otherwise send non-religious cards. Unless otherwise stated, where we say that religious cards can be sent, you can send a card of any religion without causing offence or posing a threat. When a non-religious card is advised, please avoid referring to religion in your message, e.g. rather than writing 'you are in our prayers', you could write 'you are in our thoughts'.

Around 60 people take cards from the Amnesty stall during the interval. Next Christmas, please consider sending a card to someone who is probably in solitary confinement – possibly being tortured – for his or her beliefs. How many Christians in Britain, I wonder (myself included), would 'Stand up for Jesus' when the secret police knocked on their door at midnight?

❧ Sunday 11 December

Excitement is in the air today, with everyone wanting to know the identity of the 'mystery guest' mentioned in our advert in the *Ilkley Gazette* for today's Christingle Service in aid of the Children's Society. The stranger is whisked into the church at 9 am, well before the first of 150 worshippers (60 of them children) arrive for the 9.30 am service, and is waiting in the vestry to make his grand appearance.

Before he does so, we've an unusual presentation by Catherine Gibson, who has visited the Deanery Resource Centre at Otley. The Centre's resourceful volunteers have created a long scroll depicting the Nativity story, which Catherine unrolls from the pulpit to the sound of 'Mary's Boy Child'. The young are enthralled, and I decide to arrange a repeat performance on Christmas Eve, when St Margaret's is bound to be packed.

Suddenly there's a clanging sound and in comes the mystery man, dressed in blue. He's Ilkley's town crier, Chris Richards, who helped to publicise our Christmas Fayre eight days ago in his inimitable fashion in and around the square. Chris is preceded by Fr Alan Brown carrying a large plastic Christingle, again loaned by the Resource Centre. The real Christingle oranges, to be taken home after the service, consist of … well, let Chris tell you himself:

> Oyez! Oyez! Oyez!
> We are not always very good,
> and that's why Jesus shed his blood.
> He died at Calvary on a tree
> to bridge the gap between God, you and me.
> Here in this church today we mingle
> to think about the true Christingle.
> The orange to God is of great worth –
> it's where we live: the planet Earth;
> the ribbon (smooth and O so red)
> is our nasty sins in Jesus dead;
> the sweets, which make our hearts to glow –
> the fruits of goodness which in Jesus grow.
> Come worship him, this special day,

> come let us sing our songs and pray –
> God save the Queen!

Everyone is moved by the performance, which is enough to make you tingle – Chris tingle!

Before the final blessing, Fr Alan tells the children: 'Now, these are not to be eaten in church – wait until you get them home.' Some hope! As the service ends, the young swoop on the sweets like piranhas in a Bond film.

🍀 Monday 12 December

Today I'm in London surrounded by several bishops and their wives – and a collection of dogs. We're not on the House of Bishops Annual Trip to Wimbledon Greyhound Stadium (surprisingly neglected by the press) but in the Chinese Room at Buckingham Palace for lunch with the Queen.

The Queen is in her counting-house, counting all her … corgis? They seem to be everywhere, although I am assured there are only nine:

> One's spotted five, six, seven, eight,
> where is number nine?
> Chewing the Bishop of London's trews?
> Good – all here: that's fine.

The guests are all past and present members of the Queen's Ecclesiastical Household. I'm attending as ex-Bishop of London and former Dean of the Chapels Royal with over-sight, on behalf of the Queen, of chapels including those at the Tower of London, St James's Palace and Hampton Court Palace.

The Chinese Room is magnificent, with its dragons on the ceiling and great urns, some of which Queen Victoria appreciated at Osborne House, her country retreat on the Isle of Wight. I'm not sure what the corgis are having, but the rest of us enjoy a delicious meal of smoked salmon, roast lamb and cheesecake, finishing with cheese and biscuits. As you would expect, the occasion goes like clockwork. Drinks are at 12.30 pm, and we're in the Dining Room by 1 pm. We aren't aware of being rushed, but it's all over – oh so smoothly – by 2.10 pm.

The Queen is cheerful, chatty, and obviously enjoying herself. However, not even Jeremy Paxman could persuade me to divulge anything of what's said, which to me is as confidential as anything heard during a confession. That would (in spirit at least) be treasonable, and I might have to recommend that I be sent to the Tower!

❧ Tuesday 13 December

A Quiet Day for the clergy of Otley Deanery Chapter, with about six of us at Norwood Methodist Church, near Otley. As the busiest time of the Christian year approaches, it is good to catch our breath by reflecting on Christ at various stages of his ministry. While we look at the bigger picture, there's a wonderful view through the window of trees and fields, on which sheep are eating their greens contentedly. All we (unlike sheep) have brought our sandwiches and pause for a lunchtime brew of tea and coffee.

❧ Wednesday 14 December

At 8 pm Deanery representatives from Ilkley, Ben Rhydding and Addingham meet for the first time at All Saints to discuss ways of reducing the number of paid, full-time clergy. I've said I'll only stay for an hour – if they can't make any progress in that time, they wouldn't make any in another four. As I expected, each church thinks any changes should happen elsewhere. After skirting round the knotty problems, the meeting decides to have another meeting. This issue is likely to run and run. Pray for us, St Simeon Stylites!

❧ *Thursday 15 December*

In the quaint, old-fashioned days before the *Lady Chatterley's Lover* obscenity trial in 1960, paperbacks in Britain often contained the terms 'expurgated' (cut) or 'unexpurgated' (naughty bits left in).

Following *Desert Island Discs* last Sunday, today I'm a page-3 man in the *Ilkley Gazette*, which has published an expurgated version of a press release appearing in full on our website, which highlights, not surprisingly, my choice of 'On Ilkla Moor Baht 'At'. There have been over 6,000 visitors to the website, which includes a virtual tour of St Margaret's, during the past year. The address is a mouthful, but the site can be accessed easily by searching on the internet for St Margaret's Church, Ilkley.

This afternoon I visit Homecroft care home in Victoria Avenue with Garth Kellett, Catherine Gibson and Bill Godfrey for the first of nine Christmas Carol and Communion services which we shall hold in Ilkley's care homes between now and 23 December. Parishioners who live near the homes are good about attending these services, and their presence really makes a difference to the residents. Some may not appear responsive, but it's surprising how often a well-known carol or prayer sparks off happy memories.

❧ *Saturday 17 December*

Those who grew up in the 1950s are reminded of their youth tonight when 30 girls aged nine and 10 from Moorfield

School, Ilkley, break into hand-jiving during a carol they are presenting in the annual Christmas concert by Cantores Olicanae.

The girls look seasonal in their red jumpers with black vertical stripes, red stockings and, in some cases, red ribbons in their hair. During their first carol they promise 'we will rock you', and while Baby Jesus is obviously in mind there's enough Ilkley Rock to spare for the capacity audience – even bigger, it seems, than at last week's *Messiah*.

Now how does the hand-jive go?

> clap knees
> clap hands
> twirl hands
> clench fists and hit one with the other
> put palms in elbow
> wipe nose with back of hand (sorry, that's the girl in the back row with a cold)
> hands in the air
> 'Yeah!'

Music and drama teacher Gill Jackson, who runs the choir, says they picked up the movements 'instantly'.

It's a delightful performance from Moorfield. The girls are audible and blend perfectly together, and they convey a sense of quiet, uncomplicated openness to the Gospel message about which they're singing. Cantores are in top form, too. Just over £200 is raised by a retiring collection for the Wharfe Valley Community Project, a group working with disabled and elderly local residents, so the joy of Christmas will really flow out this festive season.

❧ *Sunday 18 December*

The Lord has a way of using whatever materials are to hand, like the five barley loaves and two fish brought by a boy to Andrew (John 6:4–15). This month he has been using the feet of Tony Klepper, a server who runs the tombola at our church fairs.

'How beautiful are the feet of them that preach the gospel of peace …' (*Messiah*). Tony's plates may not seem beautiful at first sight, but they *are* size 11 ('on a good day') which is what you need when making a travelling crib.

The Playtime crib was created from one of Tony's shoe-boxes by ex-infants teacher Pat Patterson. It stayed overnight at about 15 homes during Advent, reflecting the journey which Mary and Joseph made to Bethlehem 2,000 years ago. On Friday I held a short ceremony welcoming it back with some of the 40 families currently attending Playtime. There were lots of colourful costumes as the children made their own 'journey to Bethlehem' round the church. We had two or three Marys, several Josephs – and I think four wise men! Comments about the travelling crib are displayed in church today. One thanks St Margaret's for introducing a 'half Christian, half Hindu' boy to the Christmas story:

> As 'Twinkle, Twinkle' is his favourite song, the story of the visitors' journey to the manger and the candle song proved a big hit. Whatever [he] chooses to believe when he grows up, this has been a wonderful way for him to learn what Christmas is really about.

This evening we present Carols and Readings (both sacred and secular) for Christmas, a new venture aimed at encouraging members to invite neighbours and friends to a service. Around 50 people are present – considerably more than at

Evensong normally – so the exercise should be worth repeating.

🐾 *Tuesday 20 December*

During my ministry, my faith in human nature has often been renewed by the discovery of so many people caring for others behind the scenes, with considerable grit and courage in the case of a long period of debilitating illness. Unnoticed by the newspapers are many examples of 'Heaven in ordinary'.

Carers can often feel vulnerable and isolated (especially at Christmas), but there's a local charity whose support for all kinds of carers is quite remarkable – the Carers Resource. For 10 years it has served people in Harrogate, Craven and Airedale by giving support and advice to anyone looking after someone else. Last January the charity received the Queen's Award for Voluntary Service.

More than 4,800 local carers regularly receive the Carers Resource newsletter, while about 900 carers receive sustained one-to-one support from 12 part-time carer support officers in every six-month period. In addition, more than 280 young carers (aged from seven to 18) have been assisted by the five-strong young carers team during the past four years.

I am glad to have been asked to write an article for the Christmas newsletter, as it has enabled me to pay tribute to the charity's quite invaluable work, which I hope will be mirrored elsewhere.

🐾 *Wednesday 21 December*

By coincidence this morning I visit a carer with a consider-able burden, Pam Hearnshaw, to give Holy Communion to Trevor and her mother, Mabel (97) who lives by herself in South Yorkshire with help from carers. Mabel has arrived early for Christmas after picking up a virus which left her dehydrated. She was in bed for three days, but is now downstairs and remarkably cheerful, all things considered. I also give Communion to Pam and her sister, Norma, who lives near Burnley and often helps with Trevor.

After lunch I am in church available to anyone who wants to make their Christmas confession. For the benefit of anyone who has reservations about this, it is entirely optional; just as many people like to hear their GP confirm they are freed from a physical complaint, some Anglicans feel better after hearing a priest say the words of absolution: 'By his authority committed to me, I absolve thee from all thy sins.' As I interpret it, confession via a priest is in line with the teaching of Jesus who, in Matthew 18:17, indicates that one remedy for sin is to 'tell it to the church'.

A great honour tonight is being invited to Anne Kilvington's newly resumed Meat-and-Potato-Pie Party, the local equivalent of Lord Archer's Shepherd's Pie and Krug gathering (there's no champagne at Anne's, but a good choice of wine, beer or spirits). Anne held the party from 1982 to 2000, when she was in the choir. She says of her pie: 'Quite a few people in "posh Ilkley" have said, "Oh, my grandma used to make that." So did mine.' In these days, when Christmas dinners get earlier and earlier, it's a treat not to be given white meat during an evening out!

♣ *Friday 23 December*
TICKLEMAS EVE

You could have knocked me down with a feather when I learned that my old student Father Tickle had turned down an invitation to meet Ken Dodd at St George's Hall, Bradford, which Ken has dubbed 'that Yorkshire "tribute to super-glue!".' Robert had been looking forward to Ken's Happiness

Show for several months, but at a late stage was asked to take a family funeral. I trust another opportunity will come his way. As for Ken – I hope he appreciates this 'missed Tickle' holy season.

Hugh tells me that the 'Ticklemas Eve' show is a hilarious occasion. John Hepworth, a Chairman with the Employment Tribunals Service, says watching 'the face that launched ten thousand quips' is like being on the receiving end of a machine-gun: you're just recovering from one joke when another one hits you. Part of Doddy's genius is his ability to build up a relationship with the audience within seconds. To a woman in the front row tonight who introduces herself as Pat, he says: 'I shouldn't have that embroidered on your tee-shirt.'

There are plenty of jokes about his relationship with the Inland Revenue ('Self-assessment? I invented self-assessment') and the sheer length of his shows. He pokes fun at Bradford ('not twinned with anywhere, but in a suicide pact with Grimsby'). In fact, anyone and anything is fair game during the next five hours:

> Bill Clinton takes his dog to the vet's. 'Do you think he ought to be neutered?' asks the vet. 'Yes, I'm afraid I do,' replies the dog.

At 1.10 am, an hour after the show has finally finished, Ken emerges from his dressing-room to sign autographs and chat with seven faithful fans who have waited patiently to meet him. They include a woman from Rotherham who has not missed his Bradford show in 16 years and has seen him altogether around 250 times. Next month she's due to watch him two nights running at Sheffield. What's so special about him? She thinks for five seconds. 'He's just very nice,' she says.

❧ *Saturday 24 December*
CHRISTMAS EVE

Trouble in t'vestry yesterday, when I went to check that Baby Jesus was ready to join Mary, Joseph, the Shepherds, cow and donkey at our crib, which was already in church in preparation for Carols Round the Crib, due to take place this afternoon. He wasn't – he had vanished! 'Help!' I told myself, 'Don't panic!'

Suddenly a thought flashed across my anxious mind: 'Send Fr Alan Brown to Woolies for a Baby Jesus Look-Alike, praying no reporters from the *Ilkley Gazette* are about.' Then common sense got the upper hand: 'Ring up Pam – she'll know where he is.' (Pam has looked after the crib for donkeys' years.) Phew! Apparently when Pam got the crib out from the church tower, she discovered that Jesus' right hand had come off. She was unfazed, and took him home to be mended with EvoStick! The crib is at least 30 years old, and almost every year a hand, ear, tail or some other bit has to be glued back on again. If Pam had been around for Humpty Dumpty, with her 'stickability' he might not have ended up as a giant omelette for the King's men!

So it's all smiles and moist eyes today at 4 pm, when Laura Patterson (six) fetches Baby Jesus from the altar with me and places him in the crib in front of a packed congregation (about 30 of whom are standing), enabling the youngest children to squat around the crib and sing the first verse of 'Away in a Manger' by themselves before everyone else joins in. Some of the children are on quite a long rein, but the Lord accepts people where they are and, I am sure, expects us to do likewise.

Seven hours later, around 11.45 pm, 'Silent Night' becomes a reality, as something like the 'sound of sheer silence' heard by the prophet Elijah on Mount Horeb (1 Kings 19:12)

descends. For 24 hours this deep quiet will remain, as hinted
at in 'It Came Upon the Midnight Clear':

> Yet with the woes of sin and strife
> the world has suffered long;
> beneath the angel-strain have rolled
> two thousand years of wrong;
> and man, at war with man, hears not
> the love-song which they bring:
> O hush the noise, ye men of strife,
> And hear the angels sing!

This is the peace of Emmanuel, 'God is with us'. Baby Jesus
lying in the crib may have needed help to get him to the
church on time but Jesus, eternal Word of the Father, needs
no human help in bearing the world's hurts and sorrows –
he's got the whole world in his hands. How strange: they still
bear the marks of the nails.

❧ Sunday 25 December
CHRISTMAS DAY

And Fr Alan Brown has our children in the palm of his hand
during the address at the Christmas Morning Family
Eucharist.

He's brought along a green sack, out of which he pulls
several gifts received over the years. Since the first is a family
photograph taken near Morecambe which includes 'myself in
these little shorts' [muffled guffaws from parts of the Nave],
he asks the youngsters: 'How old do you think I am now?'
When a little girl replies, all sweetness and light, '25?', the
guffawing is no longer muffled. Next Alan produces a toy
penguin ('I was attracted as a boy to the feet') and a box
containing two model buses from Accrington. All the while,

he's making cracks aimed at the adults. The last item is an icon of the Madonna and Child from a Greek Island. 'You will all enjoy unwrapping lots of lovely presents today,' Alan says, 'but God's gift of Jesus is the best Christmas present in the world.' He concludes by making everyone smile and wave towards the crib and each other.

Maybe we should lend Alan out to Ken Dodd for those moments when his throat becomes dry – like Alan's sense of humour. It's been a fine performance today, and everyone claps. Doddy is enjoying a well-earned Christmas break in Liverpool 14, but I suspect Alan's efforts have been appreciated in Heaven by Thomas, called the Twin (John 11:16) – in Greek known as 'Did[d]ymus'.

♣ Wednesday 28 December

After the joy and fun of Christmas, we come down to earth with a bang over the next three days. On Boxing Day, we remember St Stephen, the first Christian martyr (Acts 6—7), whose fearless and faithful death, some think, was an influence behind the conversion of St Paul, who witnessed it. Next day we honour John, the 'beloved' disciple, who was exiled to Patmos for his Christian witness (Revelation 1:9), while today we recall with horror the Massacre of the Innocents, murdered by Herod the 'Great' to try to remove the child reputed to be a future 'King of the Jews' (Matthew 2:1–18). Like Stephen, some Christians are dying for their faith in parts of the world today, and who knows how many innocent children are suffering as a result of God's bittersweet gift of free will?

♣ Thursday 29 December

Today we mourn the passing of Mary Wilson, lay chair of

Otley Deanery Synod and chair of the Diocesan Committee for Retired Clergy, Widows, Widowers and Dependants, who died on 20 December aged 66. Last night there was a well-attended Service of Reception, and even more people attend Mary's Funeral Requiem. The large congregation reflects Mary's wide-ranging interests, particularly in education: having been an inspirational teacher and lecturer in English Literature, she became acting co-Director of Education with Bradford Metropolitan District Council. Many people here today were friends of her late husband, Irvin, who was vicar of nearby Menston from 1982 until his death in 1987. After the service I go alone to Skipton Crematorium – Mary's family wish to say *au revoir* to her in St Margaret's, which will enable them to spend time with her friends.

❧ *Saturday 31 December*

Each to his own. Some may choose to paint the town red tonight, but I have a rare quiet evening at home by myself. My father did not believe in New Year celebrations, and we never kept the occasion as a family. I go to bed early but am wakened by a wretched firework.

January

🌑 *Sunday 1 January*
NEW YEAR'S DAY

Today's Gospel reading is about the naming and circumcision of Jesus, but might equally have been on the Parable of the Five Foolish Virgins (Matthew 25:1–13). A quarter of the congregation arrive 20 minutes late for the morning Eucharist, having failed to digest from the parish magazine and last week's pew leaflet that today's service starts at 10 am, not 10.30 am. 'Keep awake, therefore'? Some of them must have been awake too late last night and obviously slept in!

After the service, a couple of our members are among the 107 eccentrics who celebrate the New Year in traditional Ilkley manner by leaping into the bracing (6°C) spa water at White Wells, 684 ft 5 ins above sea level on Ilkley Moor. There's no charge for the 'privilege' and you can get a good cup of hot Yorkshire tea afterwards. I am not among the dippers, having been put on antibiotics by my quack for bronchitis – I had a temperature of 102°F on Monday and Tuesday.

I do recommend all those lovely swimmers loved by God to consider making the leap of faith involved in coming to a church service – and maybe even getting baptised. The water in our font is much less of a shock to the system than that at White Wells (you have to admire those totally immersing Baptists!), all that guilt for past failings can be washed away, and everything you donate for tea or coffee afterwards goes to Christian Aid.

But just for today, my New Year message (for everyone

reading this, as well as at St Margaret's) is that of today's Blessing:

> May God keep you in all your days.
> May Christ shield you in all your ways.
> May the Spirit bring you healing and peace.
> And the blessing of God Almighty,
> the Father, the Son, and the Holy Spirit
> be upon you this day
> and remain with you always!

✿ Tuesday 3 January

The Mothers' Union AGM in the hall. Not the most tempestuous of meetings, but most pacific and reasonably swift. I am in the chair. Why? A good question. Ask the Mothers' Union – the answer may be in their constitution.

✿ Friday 6 January
EPIPHANY

Today's feast celebrates the birth of Jesus not just for his fellow-Jews but for the whole world, represented by 'wise men from the East' or 'astrologers', as some manuscripts of St Matthew's Gospel put it. 'Epiphany' comes from the Greek '*epi*', 'upon', and '*phainein*', to show.

It's a time for Christians to reaffirm their commitment to the catholic Church. You'll have noted the lower-case 'c'; I'm not talking about Anglo-Catholicism, Roman Catholicism, or any other 'ism' – I am referring to the belief, set out in the Nicene Creed, in 'one holy catholic and apostolic Church'. 'Catholic' means universal, coming from the Greek '*kata*', 'throughout', and '*holos*', 'whole'.

The word should inspire the Church to be open to all – a

church which seeks, like Jesus, to welcome the outcast, the stranger and the lost; a church which, like the Christ it claims to represent, by its very nature cannot help but draw others to itself. Of course, no one will be perfect this side of death, and too often individual churches become exclusive rather than inclusive; love becomes hedged around by law; and 'church' becomes just another 'in' group for those who like that kind of thing. Wherever this happens the Christians concerned are falling short of what God intends them to be – to put it bluntly, they are sinning.

So today's feast is a clarion call to us all to be generous in our judgements about others, for in judging others, we may ourselves be judged.

✿ *Sunday 8 January*

Faites vos jeux ('place your bets') in the wager you just can't lose! According to Blaise Pascal, the seventeenth-century French philosopher, if God does not exist, doubting Thomases lose nothing by believing in him; but if God does exist, doubters gain eternal life by believing. To those who hesitate, thinking it's an even-money bet, I bring good tidings: the Father has shortened the odds in favour of those betting on his favourite, Jesus, by giving glimpses of life beyond the finishing line to those who wait on him in faith.

At today's Family Service two Betts are in the field of four for *Magi Magic*, a short play produced by St Margaret's for Epiphany. Leading the Wise Men from 'the East' (the church's west end) to the crib is the Star (Sophie Betts, aged four), with supporting actors Toby Betts (seven, gold), Barney Jones (five, frankincense) and William Jones (seven, myrrh). They are splendidly dressed; rarely can the star of wonder have been conjoined with the wonder of Woolies, as Catherine Gibson (their Director) reports:

The costumes we use were bought for Playtime – Pat Patterson spotted them in Woolworth's, at £9.99 each. They are designed for children under five, and in some cases under three, but fit our cast surprisingly well (except for a dress intended for an 'angel' of 1–2). Sophie supplies her own white dress, tights and ballet shoes but is able to use the headband, which bears a gold star on the forehead. William wears a purple cloak with an 'ermine' cape and a silver (paper) coronet; Toby is resplendent in a tunic of shiny red, blue and gold, with an exotic matching hat, to which is velcroed a grey felt beard; while Barney's tunic is of red, turquoise and silver, with matching hat and a brown felt beard. William sensibly pointed out at the costume-fitting that their trousers and tops need to be in keeping – and they are.

Catherine is surprisingly relaxed before curtain-up considering, as she puts it, that 'anything can happen'. But the Magi manage their lines well, Melchior (Barney) even confidently rejecting an Eastern tongue in favour of a West Riding accent! As the Star smiles down from the pulpit, the congregation join the Wise Men for prayers at the crib. While the riff-raff kneel on the cold, stone floor, the Magi's wives have packed kneelers for them. This is hardly surprising, since:

> Wise men, on reflection
> choose soft genuflection.

✤ *Tuesday 10 January*

A city built on a hill cannot be hidden.

(Matthew 5:14)

But St Margaret's obviously is, since many people let us know on arrival at the church that they've had difficulties in finding the way.

For many years a noticeboard giving details of our church services and activities has been situated in Back Parish Ghyll Drive, only yards from The Grove and almost opposite Ilkley's Oxfam shop. No doubt it has served its purpose, but it stuck out like a sore thumb when I first noticed it. Paint was coming off, and what remained was largely black – dark, forbidding and not a good advert for our church in an age when image is considered so important.

Tonight the PCC are told that a replacement noticeboard has arrived; it's in the vicarage garage waiting for fittings and should 'soon' be in place next to The Grove. You can imagine what that's likely to mean!

After the frantic Christmas period, I expect life to be quiet over the next week or so. Some may be rushing round the January sales, but I couldn't think of anything worse. As for booking exotic holidays – well, I always go to the same place in the North of Scotland. It hasn't yet left me bored.

❧ Sunday 15 January

Today retired clergyman Ron Barrett preaches a sermon considerably shorter than is normal at our main service, due to the enrolment of four new members of St Margaret's Mothers' Union. Oh, happy day! No offence intended to Ron: it's just that we are pleased for Carol King, a new MU member, and Elsie Short, Elaine Moorhouse and Linda Rawse, who are transferring from other branches of this family-friendly organisation – and also for Ron, who asked several weeks ago to preach on the Sunday after his birthday (without saying which it would be!).

This is Ron's way of saying thank you for the gift of life and many happy days. His sermon is based on Psalm 139 –

almost a sermon itself. In it the Psalmist acknowledges his total dependence on God from even before birth:

> For it was you who formed my inward parts;
> you knit me together in my mother's womb.
> I praise you, for I am fearfully and wonderfully made.
> Wonderful are your works;
> that I know very well ...

Ron says the psalm assures us that God knows us through and through, and is ready to support us wherever we go and whatever we do. Oh, happy news!

✤ *Monday 16 January*

One of the best prayers we could make for ourselves – after we have remembered others – is (as included in the Collect for Pentecost) to be granted 'a right judgement in all things'. St Paul seems to have had this, for whilst he could undergo 'far greater labours' than others (2 Corinthians 11:23), towards the end of his letter to the Christians at Rome he expressed a wish to visit them and 'be refreshed in your company' (Romans 15:32).

I'm not sure whether it was the pre-Christmas rush that made me develop bronchitis. That could have been nature's way of telling me to slow down, so I'm taking a break away from the parish for a week or so. Now let me see – clothes, shaving tackle, toothbrush, toothpaste, walking boots, light reading, malt whisky ... See you next week!

✤ *Monday 23 January*

> The days of our life are seventy years,
> or perhaps eighty, if we are strong ... (Psalm 90:10)

Retired clergyman Alan Millar has obviously enjoyed proving the Psalmist wrong. I return to St M's from holiday today to find people still talking about the sermon he gave yesterday, the day after he turned 80. I'm not surprised – what this optimistic octogenarian said about the miracle at Cana will probably be legendary in Ilkley when today's teenagers are 80!

According to John 2:1–11, when the wine at a wedding reception ran out, Jesus told servants to fill six large stone jars with water and give a sample to the chief steward. The water became wine, but the steward 'did not know where it came from'. Alan said one of his children had been just as ignorant about the origin of babies when his wife, Jean, was pregnant with their third child. As he was lighting a coal fire, a little voice asked where the baby had came from. Determined to be truthful, he replied: 'From a little seed in Mummy's tummy'. 'How did it get there?', the voice answered, and he responded, 'I put it there'. There was a momentary silence, followed by the crunch question: 'Did you use a shovel?' Alan told everyone that at this point it was time to retreat and use the normal adult get-out, 'We'll talk about that another time.'

As the laughter subsided (very slowly), Alan explained the point of the Gospel story today – that Jesus is still changing 'water' into 'wine'. Having overcome sin, evil and death through his Resurrection, he sends the Holy Spirit to strengthen Christians, filling them with love, joy and hope, and inspiring them to tell others about God's love for them and the world.

This was another vintage performance from Alan, to whom it might be said: 'You have kept the good wine until now.' Afterwards Alan and Jean provided wine and cake for church members, and the one child present from among their two sons and two daughters smiled at everyone as if to say: 'What makes you think it was me?'

❧ *Tuesday 24 January*

The church is packed with a varied congregation for the funeral of Jane Gilbert, a young mother who died while I was away and whose body was received into St Margaret's last night. She is escorted by friends from the Karate Club, of which she was a black belt member. Afterwards the coffin is taken to Ilkley Cemetery in a horse-drawn carriage, something I have not experienced at a funeral. I am not in the carriage but with Jane's family in the car following immediately behind.

❧ *Friday 27 January*

Today I take the regular Friday morning Shoppers' Service at Christchurch, the Methodist and United Reformed church on The Grove. We start at 10.30 am, and as the time limit is 20 minutes there's only space for a couple of hymns, a reading, some prayers, and the briefest of talks.

The sanctuary is upstairs in a large building which has been redeveloped most imaginatively since the early 1990s. It's in a prime position, so the downstairs coffee centre draws a large number of shoppers and visitors from a wide area on weekdays between 10 am and 4 pm, and on Saturdays from 10 am to noon. The church offers a listening ear on Tuesdays and Thursdays for anyone needing to talk. Many community groups use the premises, including Ilkley Council for Voluntary Service. The minister, the Revd Chris Sharp, is assisted by church and community worker Emily Hoe, who has links with other local churches; her main emphasis is on outreach with young families.

Methodists and United Reformed members work together at Christchurch under a local ecumenical partnership, worshipping as a single Christian community. Besides the traditional Sunday morning and evening services, at 9 am there is worship for today's world, 'on-line@9'. St Margaret's is fortunate to be friends with such a lively worshipping community within Churches Together in Ilkley.

❧ Saturday 28 January

If Liberal Democrat James Keeley – a real English gentleman – has been expecting our new church hall to be a heckling-free zone during his 'Immortal Memory' speech at tonight's Burns Supper, he has reckoned without Peter Cheney, a fiery Scot and Labour Party enthusiast.

Peter has already interrupted the MC, Brian Whittam, during his account of Bonnie Prince Charlie's ill-fated expedition southwards in 1745, when his exhausted troops refused to continue on towards an undefended London after they reached Derby. The Young Pretender was to prove a lost cause, rather like, some have suggested uncharitably, Peter's attempts to become a Labour councillor in diehard-Tory Ilkley. Perhaps tonight he thinks Brian is missing the buzz which only dealing with heckling can give to a politician. Brian fought three General Elections for Labour between 1966 and 1974; his best result was in 1966 at Darwen, Lancashire, where he reduced the Tory majority from 4,784 to 1,735 votes.

'As Henry VIII used to say to his wives, I'll not keep you long,' says Brian in his welcome, and soon I am delivering the traditional Selkirk Grace. Next the haggis is piped in by local reporter Jim Jack, a member of the City of Leeds Pipe Band, who is playing for the third successive year. Catherine Gibson addresses and attacks the haggis with her *sgian dubh* (like a dirk but with a shorter blade), and soon the meal arrives. Since 3.30 pm Anne Hanson's team have been busy in the kitchen preparing the tatties, neeps and haggises (shouldn't the plural be 'Haggai', like the Old Testament prophet? Never mind – so long as there's a *profit* for the church hall appeal).

James is too young to remember *Have a Go,* the wartime radio show starring Yorkshire comedian Wilfrid Pickles, but he adopts this policy in his speech, which is well received even by Peter. Labour, Conservatives ... even his own LibDems get a good teasing from this likeable lawyer, as does Respect MP George Galloway, recently evicted from Channel 4's *Celebrity Big Brother.* I had better not elaborate on the link which James makes between 'Gorgeous' George, his *Big Brother* leotard and the Weapons of Mass Destruction, since we still have to pay towards the hall's costs a sizeable proportion of the sum which George was awarded against the *Daily Telegraph* in libel damages, and we don't want to start fund-raising again.

Everyone is cheerful, but as not even the handful of Scots present are prepared to read any Burns poems (the first time this has happened), we sing more Scots songs than at any of the four previous Burns Suppers, only having problems when pianist Godfrey Higgins 'does a Les Dawson' during the final number. Of course, in addition to the Scots songs we manage all eight verses of 'On Ilkla Moor Baht 'At'. Just before going-home time, the raffle is drawn, and Barbara France wins back the box of French chocolates she had left over from Christmas. She hands it back and it's won by a Scottish lady, who is delighted at the prospect of saving a few pounds, while Anne is pleased to have 'put on' £577 for the parish hall fund. Organising a meal for around 100 would tire most people, but Anne, a former civil servant in the Department for Work and Pensions, has bags of energy. In 2004, with her husband Malcolm, a former police inspector, she walked the 100-mile length of Hadrian's Wall in aid of the hall appeal. They spent a pleasant evening at a farm near Housesteads Fort with former DJ Noel Edmonds ('very fit and very nice – not a bit stand-offish', says Anne). How might the course of British history

have been altered, I wonder, if through the mist of a cold
November morning the Romans had seen advancing towards
them warriors led by the wild-eyed Hamish McBlobby?

𝕾 *Sunday 29 January*

> And lead us not into temptation; but deliver us from
> evil …

'Lead' and 'temptation' went together, unfortunately, like eggs
on to a plate in a young man helped by Fr Alan Brown around
20 years ago.

I don't mean 'lead' (verb), 'to show the way by going first'
(Chambers Dictionary), but 'lead' (noun)– 'a well-known soft
bluish-grey metal'. The 16-year-old had been convicted of
stealing the metal and, Alan believes, almost certainly knew
more about the roofs of churches than the interior of the
buildings.

In today's sermon Alan says that as an NHS general manager he visited the teenager at the Spinal Injuries Unit in
Sheffield. The young man had fractured his spine in an accident at a gym and would never move his arms or legs again.
He would not feel hunger either, having lost all feeling in his
stomach. He was astonished to meet Alan, since no one had
ever travelled 50 miles just for him. 'Underneath it all, he was
quite a nice lad,' adds Alan. 'Perhaps he would have stayed out
of trouble if he had been valued earlier in life – as it is, he felt
worthless.'

Alan says we should be wary about judging anyone, since
'demons' are in us all. However, Christ can cast out doubts
and fears from the dark recesses of anyone's being. Having
received his love in the Word of the Gospel and the Sacrament
of Holy Communion, Christians must take it out so that others may perhaps receive healing and peace.

✣ *Tuesday 31 January*

For the first time, the Deanery Synod meets at St Margaret's new hall. Succeeding Mary Wilson as lay chair is Mrs Marilyn Banister, who conducts the business so efficiently that we finish on time at 9.30 pm – something like a record for the Church of England!

February

✤ Wednesday 1 February

After Morning Prayer, I suddenly remember at 8.30 am that I am to host today's ecumenical clergy lunch. I'm not a hoarder, so there's nothing for it but to get straight off to Tesco and fight my way to the fresh soup counter through the myriads of schoolchildren buying Mars Bars, crisps and other things which they shouldn't be eating. Sadly, the soup fridge has failed, so I head for the tinned soup area and select three large tins of Heinz Tomato Soup (perhaps I shouldn't have been so specific). I also choose two of Tesco's delicious (I'm back in favour) large freshly baked loaves, cheese and cranberry fruit drink.

[Since this entry was written, Mick Carr, Tesco's manager at Ilkley, has arranged for all the store's fridges to be renewed. Now that I think about it, there's a mini-sermon here. Like cars, fridges, TV sets – everything sold in our stores – we all get worn down at times by daily life and long to be renewed. A holiday often helps, though of course things can go wrong even then! But many will testify to God's inexhaustible power to refresh and renew ('be transformed by the renewing of your minds,' St Paul advises in Romans 12:2). God cares about everyone who works and shops at all our stores, despite the introduction of Sunday trading.]

✤ Thursday 2 February

Tonight the choir and about 30 parishioners light candles at the start of a service marking an underrated Christian feast-day, Candlemas. It recalls how the Virgin Mary was ritually purified and then presented Jesus, her first-born son, in the Temple at Jerusalem in obedience to Jewish religious law (Luke 2:22–40). The term Candlemas was adopted later due to the custom by which candles for use in church services throughout the next 12 months were blessed on this day. Today the emphasis is on Jesus as Light of the World.

> … God is light and in him there is no darkness at all.
> (1 John 1:5)

Our candles remind us that this Light came among us as man and that the darkness of this world's wickedness, strife and evil will never overcome it. You may recall the painting by Holman Hunt which hangs in St Paul's Cathedral. Jesus stands at the door – the door of the life of everyone who comes into the world. But there is no handle on the *outside*. It is up to us whether we open up and allow our lives to be flooded with the light, life and love which Christ offers to all.

Importantly, there is a mission dimension to this feast. Jesus says to every Christian, '*You* are the light of the world …' (Matthew 5:14). Each of us is challenged to reflect something of the light who is Jesus Christ in all that we are and do. It may sometimes be in big ways, but more likely in the small and the ordinary that, as St Francis puts it, we may become channels of Christ's light, love, peace and joy.

❧ Friday 3 February

To Skipton Building Society for another charitable foundation meeting. It's heartening to see how many initiatives there are by local voluntary groups and organisations to improve the lives of others, for example, disabled children. Today we make grants to 12 organisations totalling around £23,000. Of course there's a bit of advertising involved, but there's more to it than that – some of the original philanthropic principles remain embodied in the Society, which genuinely wants to give something back to the community. You have to be pretty soulless to give mammon (Matthew 6:24) absolute priority!

❧ *Sunday 5 February*

Following Jesus took a lot out of the apostles. After the missionary trip recorded in Mark 6, they were so tired that Jesus told them to take a break, but within hours they were helping him to feed a huge crowd, which probably drained both him and them.

Today's Gospel reading (Mark 1:29–39) records how, after a period at the start of his ministry, Jesus rose before dawn to recharge his batteries through prayer. If *he* was refreshed in this way, so can we be. Many people find the ACTS prayer method (Adoration, Confession, Thanksgiving, Supplication) helpful, but sometimes it is good simply to rest in God after a short Bible reading, saying few words or none, as though by a pool of still water. At other times, a routine of prayer for, say, 10 minutes first thing each morning can make the rest of the day go that bit better. Those who are in touch with the Lord are likely to be more in tune with their work colleagues and others!

❧ *Monday 6 February*

> When Irish eyes are smiling, sure it's like a morning
>   spring,
> In the lilt of Irish laughter, you can hear the angels
>   sing ...

There will be lots of smiling Irish faces at the Yeats Country

Hotel at Rosses Point, County Sligo, where I'm to lead an away day for clergy from the Church of Ireland's Dublin Diocese over the next few days. Many of the clergy will be pleased to be present, since they are normally pretty isolated in rural areas of Ireland.

After an early morning flight from Leeds-Bradford Airport, I'm met at Dublin by the Archbishop of Dublin, John Neil. We get into his car and head for Sligo, just over three hours away. After an hour, we stop at a roadside café for a bowl of soup, cup of tea and comfort stop, then we're on the road again, arriving at the hotel at 3.40 pm. The Yeats is a traditional Irish hotel – the décor is somewhat over-heavy, but as you'd expect the staff are cheerful and welcoming and the food is bound to be good.

We've cut it rather fine, as my first presentation is at 4 pm – on the theme of 'Priesthood: Pain or Pleasure?' Yes, you're right – it's a bit of both. The pleasure comes from trying to take the Lord's love to everyone we come across; the pain comes when you lot don't always react how we would like you to – sometimes because you expect too much of us. Jesus had the same problem, so in our better moments we know we're in good company and being a priest is a privilege. After dinner, pleasure of a different sort is available as the hotel bar is well stocked. Quite a bit of drink is downed both sides of midnight. It's not quite like *Father Ted*, but some of my colleagues are planning to have Lucozade as morning chasers, since apparently it's the latest thing for hangovers. Priests are human, too, as the absolution following Confession makes clear: 'Go in peace and pray for me, a sinner too.'

♣ *Tuesday 7 February*

This morning I give two more hour-long presentations on words from the Ordination Service: 'Steward, watchman and messenger of the Lord', reflecting on how they relate to our ministry to the Church and the world. I'm planning to walk after lunch along the wild Atlantic coast but there's a gale and heavy rain. Fortunately Robert MacCarthy, the Dean of St Patrick's Cathedral, kindly invites a couple of us to accompany him on an enjoyable tour of Lissadell, one of Ireland's grandest houses on the shore of Sligo Bay. In the evening I assist the Archbishop at a service of Holy Communion with the Laying-on of Hands or Anointing for those who wish it. Dinner afterwards at the Waterfront Restaurant. I imagine everyone will have an early night tonight, with cocoa a popular nightcap!

❧ *Wednesday 8 February*

My final presentation has to be streamlined in view of the long drive back to Dublin. We dash into the car and are at the Airport by 1.15 pm. The plane takes off at 3 pm, and I land at Leeds-Bradford 40 minutes later, in good time for Evensong at St Margaret's at 6 pm.

❧ *Thursday 9 February*

Hold page 9 – today I contribute the 'Thought for the Week' article in the *Ilkley Gazette*. My theme, exterior and interior gloom, follows several days of 'anticyclonic gloom': those days when it hardly gets light and a haze descends all day.

Here are the highlights and, despite what people often say about newspapers, I am confident that I haven't misquoted myself:

> … And the cold and the gloom can and does affect the personalities of some people very seriously. Even for most of us a dull day is not exactly the most exciting

prospect. It can and does have its dulling effects in a
whole variety of ways. Add to that the seemingly
constant stream of bad news stories: yet another suicide
bombing in Iraq, a further crisis in the supply of oil, a
young person brutally murdered almost on one's own
doorstep (or so it feels, such is the power and immedia-
cy of present day communications). Something happens
in one part of the world and it is there before us in our
sitting rooms and kitchens almost simultaneously.

Down the ages many Christian writers have reflect-
ed on their journey through life, the experience that
they have had of their Christian faith and the way in
which it has interacted with their daily lives. And for
some, far from being straightforward, uncomplicated
and undemanding, they have experienced it as a constant struggle, as darkness rather than light and as
unknowing rather than knowing, such is the paradox of
Christian experience.

One thing though is certain, that even on the dark-
est and gloomiest of days something as ordinary and
straightforward as a smile towards another person can
be a real tonic. So, too, can a cheerful word of encouragement, a visit to a neighbour for a chat, an arm round
a shoulder or the holding of a hand or simply taking
the trouble to be with another person – all of these are
ways in which as human beings we can light up each
others' lives.

The English priest-poet, George Herbert, uses the
phrase 'Heaven in ordinary'. And that's absolutely right,
for whether the day is bright or dark, it's in the
ordinary things of life, our daily situations and circumstances, that we discover the possibility of 'Heaven in
ordinary' – that is if each one of us really is committed
to the brightening of another's day, which even on the

gloomiest of days brings cheer, encouragement and hope.

🎕 *Friday 10 February*

However irksome life can be in Britain, usually we are simply not aware how lucky we are, as an e-mail received from Nepal makes clear.

It's from Dr Digby Hoyal, brother of Fr Richard, who as director of the Tansen United Mission Hospital saved Kamala Bhattarai and her four children from chronic poverty and despair in 2002 after he and his wife Anne discovered them living in a hovel made from branches and corrugated iron pieces. Kamala had crushing debts and was working 12 hours a day carrying bread around for only 30p a day. With help from Anglicans in the Bradford Diocese, Digby paid off the debts and bought a cottage with two acres of farmland for the family.

Sadly, Nepal has faced an escalating political crisis since King Gyanendra seized full power a year ago, with widespread violence by Maoist terrorists bringing parts of the country to the brink of anarchy.

Digby, now retired and living in Australia, says that only two months ago he and Anne were able to travel freely in Nepal, but the recent elections (seen by the opposition as aimed at justifying the King's actions) had stirred up 'massive' demonstrations in Kathmandu.

He adds: 'The attack last week by Maoists on Tansen town has brought disaster to that community. We hear that in spite of many deaths and injuries on both sides, and the bombing and burning in the old town, at present our folk are OK.'

At Digby's request, we shall make special prayers for Tansen, their friends, and indeed the whole of Nepal.

❧ *Monday 13 February*

> A life on the ocean wave,
> A home on the rolling deep ...
>
> The sea is his, for he made it ... (Psalm 95:5)

Ask anyone who buys lottery tickets what they dream of doing if they win, and a large proportion will surely say 'go on a world cruise', for such a holiday has all most people could wish for – exotic destinations, fabulous food, non-stop entertainment ... and a chance to get away from everyone and everything.

Fr Bernard Gribbin (71) and his wife, Betty, returned home yesterday from a round-the-world trip on the P and O luxury liner *Artemis*. They indeed escaped from everyone, except the Lord Jesus. For on six Sundays at sea, after the Captain's service (based largely on the Book of Common Prayer), Bernard celebrated Holy Communion for 80–100 people. 'I wouldn't call it a "busman's holiday" – it was a great pleasure to be of service,' he says.

Bernard and Betty left Southampton on Sunday 25 October, and stopped at 43 ports in about 25 countries on a journey equivalent to 42,000 land miles, travelling via Rio de Janeiro, the Falkland Islands, Australia, New Zealand, Los Angeles, Mexico and the Panama Canal. Among the highlights was a visit to the Christ the Redeemer statue overlooking Rio. 'It was misty, so the Lord kept appearing and disappearing, which added to the sense of mystery. It reminded me of the Transfiguration,' Bernard says.

There was no post-Falklands War hostility towards Britain in Argentina, but the Falkland Islanders were pleased to meet the *Artemis'* passengers, who were struck by the tiny houses, bleak surroundings, and in Port Stanley a neat row of bungalows with a street sign reading Thatcher Drive. In Australia Bernard was moved by a reunion with his younger brother, Gordon, and sister, Pauline, whom he had not seen for nearly 30 years. Nearing home, the couple were fascinated by a 30-mile trip through the Panama Canal. 'It took eight to 10 hours to go through – the locks are enormous, able to take ships of 100,000 tonnes.'

The couple ate up the information supplied in lecturers about the countries being visited, but had to be self-disciplined when it came to the non-stop food. 'We had to refuse much of the beautiful freshly baked bread – but didn't turn down the puddings,' Betty confesses.

In view of all that lovely temptation, Bernard and Betty are to be congratulated on only gaining four or five pounds each in weight. I bet they're glad Lent is on the horizon!

✣ Tuesday 14 February

This morning the new Dean of Bradford Cathedral, David Ison, meets the Otley Deanery Chapter at All Saints, explaining his views and ideas for the cathedral. It's helpful for both him and us to get to know each other – hopefully a new chapter for the cathedral will help to breathe new life into the Chapter!

✣ Thursday 16 February

Tonight I'm back with United Reformed Christians again, this time at the Bridge Church in Otley. At great inexpense I'm addressing the Men's Club, but since I'm still rather a curiosity around here they've invited the ladies as well. I give my usual talk on 'The See', which they seem to find edifying and educational. Afterwards , there's the usual ritual of pie and peas.

♣ *Sunday 19 February*

Anyone who gives even a passing glance to the New Testament must realise it does not tell us the whole truth about Jesus. What did he look like? What *was* he like (as opposed to the different pictures of him presented in each of the four Gospels)? The last question has occupied and eluded scholars down the centuries, because it is almost certainly impossible to separate fact and interpretation in the Gospels.

In today's sermon I suggest it will never be possible to pin down the real Jesus. I don't say 'Am I bovvered?', but that's what it boils down to. For does it really matter? Do we need to know the shape of his face, the colour of his eyes, style of his hair and so on? Surely such matters are mere details in the context of the amazing belief which both John 1:1–14 and Colossians 1:15–20 declare about the nature and person of Jesus – that mystery enshrined in the Nicene Creed: 'And was incarnate from the Holy Spirit and the Virgin Mary and was made man.'

John's Gospel gives no pictorial account of the birth of Jesus such as those in Matthew and Luke, with the angels, shepherds and wise men. But here is a theological statement of the most profound kind:

> In the beginning was the Word ... And the Word became flesh and lived among us, and we have seen his glory, the glory as of a father's only son, full of grace and truth.

Jesus, according to John, is nothing less than God and has come from being with God in the beginning. St Paul claims that it is in the visible Jesus that we see the invisible God. As one scholar puts it: 'To see what God is like, we must look at Jesus.' Another, more recent, scholar writes: 'Jesus is the human face of God.'

The Gospels themselves are the best written testimony to Jesus, but what we celebrate today and every Sunday in church is the presence – the real presence of the living Lord in the power of his Holy Spirit; that presence which has been recognised and celebrated week by week by successive generations of Christians. Through the reading of the Gospel and the breaking of bread at each Eucharist, Jesus Christ is in our midst speaking again words of comfort, encouragement and challenge, giving us fresh hope for the future – just as he apparently gave to the great German theologian, doctor and missionary Albert Schweitzer (1875–1965), who concluded his *The Quest of the Historical Jesus* (published in English, 1910) as follows:

> Jesus as a concrete historical personality remains a stranger to our time, but His spirit, which lies hidden in His words, is known in simplicity, and its influence is direct ... The names in which men expressed their recognition of Him [as an authoritative ruler], Messiah, Son of Man, Son of God, have become for us historical parables. We can find no designation which expresses what He is for us ... [but] He comes to us as One unknown, without a name, as of old, by the lake-side, He came to those men who knew Him not. He speaks to us the same word: 'Follow thou me!' and sets us to the tasks which He has to fulfil for our time. He commands. And to those who obey Him, whether they be wise or simple, He will reveal Himself in the toils, the conflicts, the sufferings which they shall pass through in His fellowship, and, as an ineffable mystery, they shall learn in their own experience Who He is.

❧ Monday 20 February

My day off, and a meeting with my fellow directors of
Parcevall Hall, near Appletreewick, the Diocesan Retreat
House and Conference Centre. We are responsible for the
house and estate, which draws many visitors – it has some
unique specimens of shrub and flower. The house is in the
Yorkshire Dales National Park, and the authorities have had a
field day with restrictions and regulations. Will there be a
reaction against all this one day? At Bishopthorpe there was a
sign on the terrace by the river reading: 'Danger – Deep
Water'. I was tempted to add: 'Suitable only for Baptists'.

❧ Saturday 25 February

> Onward, Christian soldiers, marching as to war,
> with the cross of Jesus going on before …

That's all very well for us young 'uns, but not always so easy
when you're over 80 and have osteoarthritis. Trevor Gibbons
(85) can manage to walk upstairs ('one step at a time, sweet
Jesus') but goes down backwards, the only way his knees can
cope with the strain. So when he leaves church, strengthened
by God's Holy Spirit, it's a case for him of 'backwards,
Christian soldier'.

Trevor sees himself as rather like the Church of England –
sometimes looking forward; sometimes back. Although he is
'catholic and conservative', he feels Anglican worship must be
made more appealing to young people, the Church's future.
Inward-looking concerns are a distraction in comparison
with the overriding objective of waiting upon God's love and
taking it 'out there'. Trevor was a friend of the late Rt Revd
Kenneth Giggall, Bishop of St Helena, who when the issue of
women priests arose joked that one day an Archbishop of

Canterbury might wish to marry an Archbishop of York!

(Trevor died on 25 October 2006. His family has long been associated with St Margaret's; the magnificent reredos designed by his uncle, J.H. Gibbons, will continue to evoke happy memories of this well-liked man.)

✣ *Sunday 26 February*

> We will … all be changed, in a moment, in the twinkling of an eye, at the last trumpet.
>
> (1 Corinthians 15:52)

Fr Alan Brown will never forget the day when he could so easily have been 'changed' – under the wheels of a Citroën or a Peugeot in Paris last week.

It happened (or didn't happen) as he walked with hardly a care in the world along the Rue Jacob towards the Musée d'Orsay to view its great collection of Impressionist paintings. Suddenly, at the junction of two streets, his left ankle gave way on a patch of uneven ground and he was propelled on to a road on which cars normally rush past. 'By God's good providence there was not one car coming, or there would probably not have been a sermon today by me – or ever,' he tells startled church members today.

Alan says that as he lay on the ground, forced into aware-ness of his fragility, for a few brief moments time slowed down, and afterwards he could recall every stage in the inci-dent. He likens his experience to that of Peter, James and John at Jesus' Transfiguration (Mark 9:2–9) – something spectacu-lar was happening around them which they were not able to control. But he adds: 'Despite the smallness of our lives, if we are held in God's transforming power, we can be changed and take something of that power – that love – out for others.'

❧ *Monday 27 February*

> Give us this day our daily bread …

A good prayer to make tonight before retiring to bed, on what might perhaps be dubbed White Uncut Monday. By 9 pm, three hours before closing, only three sliced loaves remain on the shelves at Tesco in Ilkley.

Why this lack of consumer confidence? A leap in world wheat prices? A terrorist threat or imminent lorry drivers' blockade? No – talk of snow on the horizon. Don't panic-buy, everyone: bread will doubtless be back on the shelves tomorrow morning and, if it isn't, Tesco is packed with other items such as Maria Theresa's favourite, cake. At the church hall tomorrow night pancakes (both sweet and savoury) will be served at a quiz night to mark the eve of Lent.

❧ *Tuesday 28 February*

> Q: What remark did Violet Elizabeth Bott make to William Brown which made the Outlaw yield to her soppy, girlish requests?

That's the first question set by David and Patsy Glover in tonight's quiz night. Not everyone has read Richmal Crompton's *William* books, but quite a few have seen Bonnie Langford as Violet Elizabeth on TV so most know the answer. Not all are aware that the remark is recorded in slightly different forms in *William in Trouble* and *Still William*, the latter giving:

> ''F you don' play houth with me, I'll thcream n' thcream till I'm thick. I can,' she added with pride.

You might expect a roomful of Christians to know how many King Herods appear in the New Testament – 1, 2, 3 or 4? But not many do – the answer is 4:

1. Herod the Great, who massacred the Innocents (Matthew 2:1–18);
2. Herod Antipas, who had John the Baptist executed (Mark 6:14–29) and mocked Jesus (Luke 23:7–11);
3. Herod Agrippa I, who imprisoned Peter and beheaded James (Acts 12:1–3);
4. Herod Agrippa II, whom St Paul addressed (Acts 26).

There's much joviality when it's announced that Table 7 have only remembered three Herods, since the team includes Fr Graham Sanders and me. We seem to have merged the Agrippas, and of course someone just has to say: 'Get a grip on yourselves!'

Table 1 can hardly laugh at us, for in the mystery photographs question they spend 10 minutes arguing whether a particular celebrity is Lee Westwood or Tiger Woods. In fact it's Zara Phillips (to be fair to Zara, it's not a good photo!). For a time they are also convinced that a distinguished-looking moustachioed gentleman is Dr Crippen, when in fact it's Sir Edward Elgar.

Table 7 are joint third, but Table 2, including Garth and Maggie Kellett, are declared the winners. This leaves them with another tricky question. Should they leave their prize of chocolates until Easter Day? If not, they'll have to scoff the lot before midnight, and after all those pancakes, there's a danger that Pancake Day will turn into VE Day – Violet Elizabeth Day.

Sick transit – gloria!

Postscript

Saturday 28 October

It has been a busy but rewarding time for me at Ilkley. I had hoped to be Priest-in-Charge of St Margaret's for five years, but as all those Burns enthusiasts who enjoyed a wonderful evening in our new hall back in January will be aware:

> The best laid schemes o' mice an' men
> gang aft a-gley.

On medical advice I was away from the parish from May until the end of August. I returned on 1 September, but on the advice of Bishop David cut down to a three-day week. My consultant had warned me against doing five days' work in three and, after much thought and prayer, later in the month I announced my decision to resign before the end of the year.

The news came as a shock to many, but there's a good spirit at St Margaret's and I am sure they will adapt and look forward. As I write, a new lighting scheme is being introduced, and soon new glass doors will be installed in memory of Leonard Darley, a loyal church member who was a churchwarden and chair of the Diocesan Advisory Committee. My chief wish for the parishioners is that they will continue to reflect on a challenge which I issued at two mission days: how to be more effective as the Church in the community. Above all, how is St Margaret's to reach out to the young, the Church both of today and of tomorrow?

During my ministry I have often found that when a door

closes, a window opens before long. The Lord has been a 'God of surprises', and I look forward with eager anticipation and excitement to what he has in store for me. No doubt I'll have to develop an altogether different style in that ministry to which I believe myself to have been called, namely a share in the missionary priesthood of Jesus Christ. Perhaps I'll lead a retreat once a year and the occasional pilgrimage. I should like to give some addresses, but these will be strictly limited. My immediate priority will be a period of quiet in which I can be open to God's guidance.

No one is immune from suffering, yet I am quite sure with St Paul that nothing 'will be able to separate us from the love of God in Christ Jesus our Lord' (Romans 8:39). So let you and I continue on life's road with hope (that word again!), while being thankful for many everyday blessings.

May God bless and keep you and all those whom you love – today and always!